SUPPLEMENT TO THE PRESIDENT'S BUDGET
FOR FISCAL YEAR 2015

THE NETWORKING AND INFORMATION TECHNOLOGY RESEARCH AND DEVELOPMENT PROGRAM

March 24, 2014

Members of Congress:

I am pleased to transmit the FY 2015 annual report of the Federal Government's multiagency Networking and Information Technology Research and Development (NITRD) Program. The NITRD Program, which today comprises 20 member agencies and many additional participating agencies, coordinates Federal research and development investments in advanced digital technologies that are essential for the Nation's economic growth and prosperity. NITRD agencies collaborate closely in the planning and execution of their respective research programs, leveraging Federal investments in a highly coordinated manner that enables the Program as a whole to have greater positive impact than agencies could achieve working alone.

Networking and information technologies have transformed the lives of all Americans and revolutionized capabilities across the globe for business, government, and education. Advances in digital technologies have been key to U.S. economic growth, innovation, and job creation, and will be essential to continued progress in developing new capabilities in domains such as the sciences, national security, manufacturing, education, energy, transportation, and education.

President Obama has emphasized that networking and computing capabilities will also provide critical foundations for a number of key priorities, including increasing the efficiency and effectiveness of the healthcare system; developing sustainable energy sources and energy delivery systems; and ensuring a resilient, secure Internet.

Federal NITRD investments made today will be crucial to the creation of tomorrow's new industries and workforce opportunities. I look forward to continuing to work with you to support this vital Federal program.

Sincerely,

John P. Holdren
Director and
Assistant to the President for Science and Technology

Contents

Introduction

The Networking and Information Technology Research and Development (NITRD) Program is the Nation's primary source of Federally funded work on advanced information technologies in computing, networking, and software. The multiagency NITRD Program seeks to:

- Provide research and development foundations for assuring continued U.S. technological leadership in advanced networking, computing systems, software, and associated information technologies

- Provide research and development foundations for meeting the needs of the Federal Government for advanced networking, computing systems, software, and associated information technologies

- Accelerate development and deployment of these technologies in order to maintain world leadership in science and engineering; enhance national defense and national and homeland security; improve U.S. productivity and competitiveness and promote long-term economic growth; improve the health of the U.S. citizenry; protect the environment; improve education, training, and lifelong learning; and improve the quality of life

The NITRD Program provides Federal agencies with effective mechanisms for sharing information and coordinating cross-agency investments in networking and information technology research and development. From supercomputers to smart phones, high-speed optical networks to mobile body area networks, and robots to innovative neurotechnologies for the brain, the NITRD Program has supported the Federal Government's mission of sponsoring and investing in fundamental networking and information technology research.

In January 2013 the President's Council of Advisors on Science and Technology (PCAST) released the report, *Designing a Digital Future: Federally Funded Research and Development in Networking and Information Technology*,[1] in which it stated:

> "The impact of networking and information technology (NIT) is stunning. Virtually every human endeavor is affected as advances in NIT enable or improve domains such as scientific discovery, human health, education, the environment, national security, transportation, manufacturing, energy, governance, and entertainment. NIT is also a powerful engine of economic growth."

The PCAST report underscores the pivotal role that sustained investment in fundamental NIT research and development has played in establishing U.S. leadership in advanced information technologies and in fueling the NIT innovations that propel the global economy and the critical infrastructure upon which modern life depends.

The FY 2015 budget guidance on science and technology priorities from OMB and OSTP included investments in big data and cybersecurity R&D.[2] The budget requests by NITRD agencies in the FY 2015 Supplement align with OMB-OSTP guidance. Examples of this include:

Big Data: This past year, NITRD's Big Data Senior Steering Group (SSG) had a key role in the White House event, "Data to Knowledge to Action: Building New Partnerships," which highlighted big data accomplishments and the importance of multi-stakeholder partnerships across government, industry, academia, and non-profit organizations. The National Science Foundation's solicitation "Critical Techniques and Technologies for Advancing Big Data Science and Engineering" and the National Institutes of Health's "Big Data to Knowledge" initiative, which launched last year, are examples of funding that align Federal agency and Administration priorities and that benefited from agency participation in the activities of the Big Data SSG.

---

[1] *Designing a Digital Future: Federally Funded Research and Development in Networking and Information Technology*. Report to the President and Congress, January 2013: http://www.whitehouse.gov/sites/default/files/microsites/ostp/pcast-nitrd2013.pdf

[2] Office of Management and Budget - Office of Science and Technology Policy Memorandum on Science and Technology Priorities for the FY 2015 Budget (M-13-16), July 26, 2013: http://www.whitehouse.gov/sites/default/files/microsites/ostp/fy_15_memo_m-13-16.pdf

Cybersecurity R&D: Cybersecurity R&D continued to be a priority focus area for the Administration and NITRD agencies, as indicated by the agencies' strategic investments in cybersecurity R&D and the completion of a NITRD report this past year on the Federal response to implementing the 2011 Federal Cybersecurity R&D Strategic Plan.[3]

Cyber-Physical Systems: A focus on cyber-physical systems R&D continues to gain traction with the Cyber Physical Systems Senior Steering Group (CPS SSG) and High Confidence Software and Systems Coordinating Group sponsoring a series of workshops on multidisciplinary, cyber-physical systems R&D needs. Based on CPS SSG collaborations, the group has developed and issued a joint solicitation on fundamental cyber-physical systems research.

Social Computing: The NITRD/NCO has also given focus to social computing by recently forming a Social Computing Team under the Social, Economic, and Workforce Implications of IT, and IT Workforce Development (SEW) program component area. The Social Computing Team held its first workshop, "Social Computing and Crisis Management," this past summer and a workshop on "Social Computing and Gaming" this spring.

Privacy R&D: Privacy has increasingly emerged as a focus area for the Administration and the public. The NITRD Program has responded by initiating a collaborative effort to develop the scientific and engineering foundations of privacy R&D. At the request of the Office of Science and Technology Policy (OSTP), the NITRD/NCO has been collecting information from NITRD agencies about their research activities in privacy. The information will be used to assess current and planned Federal R&D activities in support of privacy in cyberspace, identify opportunities for multiagency coordination and initiatives, and explore a possible research agenda in the foundations of privacy.

For further information about these NITRD efforts, please see the NITRD website: http://www.nitrd.gov.

---

[3] *Trustworthy Cyberspace: Strategic Plan for the Federal Cybersecurity Research and Development Program,* December 2011: http://www.whitehouse.gov/sites/default/files/microsites/ostp/fed_cybersecurity_rd_strategic_plan_2011.pdf

NITRD Member Agencies

The following Federal agencies conduct or support R&D in advanced networking and information technologies, report their IT research budgets in the NITRD crosscut, and provide support for program coordination:

Department of Commerce (DOC)
    National Institute of Standards and Technology (NIST)
    National Oceanic and Atmospheric Administration (NOAA)
Department of Defense (DoD)
    Defense Advanced Research Projects Agency (DARPA)
    National Security Agency (NSA)
    Office of the Secretary of Defense (OSD)
    Service Research Organizations (Air Force, Army, Navy)
Department of Energy (DOE)
    National Nuclear Security Administration (DOE/NNSA)
    Office of Electricity Delivery and Energy Reliability (DOE/OE)
    Office of Science (DOE/SC)
Department of Health and Human Services (HHS)
    Agency for Healthcare Research and Quality (AHRQ)
    National Institutes of Health (NIH)
    Office of the National Coordinator for Health Information Technology (ONC)
Department of Homeland Security (DHS)
Environmental Protection Agency (EPA)
National Aeronautics and Space Administration (NASA)
National Archives and Records Administration (NARA)
National Reconnaissance Office (NRO)
National Science Foundation (NSF)

NITRD Participating Agencies

The following Federal agencies participate in NITRD activities and have mission interests that involve applications and R&D in advanced networking and information technologies:

Department of Commerce (DOC)
    National Telecommunications and Information Administration (NTIA)
Department of Defense (DoD)
    Defense Information Systems Agency (DISA)
    Intelligence Advanced Research Projects Activity (IARPA)
    Military Health System (MHS)
    Telemedicine and Advanced Technology Research Center (TATRC)
Department of Education (ED)
Department of Energy (DOE)
    Advanced Research Projects Agency-Energy (ARPA-E)
Department of Health and Human Services (HHS)
    Centers for Disease Control and Prevention (CDC)
    Centers for Medicare and Medicaid Services (CMS)
    Food and Drug Administration (FDA)
    Indian Health Service (IHS)
    Office of the Assistant Secretary for Preparedness and Response (ASPR)
Department of Interior (Interior)
    U.S. Geological Survey (USGS)
Department of Justice (DOJ)
    Federal Bureau of Investigation (FBI)
    National Institute of Justice (NIJ)
Department of State (State)
Department of Transportation (DOT)
    Federal Aviation Administration (FAA)
    Federal Highway Administration (FHWA)
Department of the Treasury (Treasury)
    Office of Financial Research (OFR)
Department of Veterans Affairs (VA)
Federal Communications Commission (FCC)
General Services Administration (GSA)
National Transportation Safety Board (NTSB)
Nuclear Regulatory Commission (NRC)
Office of the Director of National Intelligence (ODNI)
U.S. Agency for International Development (USAID)
U.S. Bureau of Labor Statistics (BLS)
U.S. Department of Agriculture (USDA)

The NITRD Program

About the NITRD Program

Now in its 23rd year, NITRD is one of the oldest and largest of the formal Federal programs that engage multiple agencies. As required by the High-Performance Computing Act of 1991 (P.L. 102-194), the Next Generation Internet Research Act of 1998 (P.L. 105-305), and the America COMPETES (Creating Opportunities to Meaningfully Promote Excellence in Technology, Education, and Science) Act of 2007 (P.L. 110-69), NITRD provides a framework and mechanisms for coordination among the Federal agencies that support advanced IT R&D and report IT research budgets in the NITRD crosscut. Many other agencies with IT interests also participate informally in NITRD activities.

Agencies coordinate their NITRD research activities and plans in Program Component Areas (PCAs). The PCAs are identified as an Interagency Working Group (IWG) or a Coordinating Group (CG) and report their R&D budgets as a crosscut of the NITRD agencies. They are charged with facilitating interagency program planning, developing and periodically updating interagency roadmaps, developing recommendations for establishing Federal policies and priorities, summarizing annual activities for the NITRD Program's Supplement to the President's Budget, and identifying potential opportunities for collaboration that have been identified by the Office of Management and Budget (OMB) and the Office of Science and Technology Policy (OSTP) as priorities for Federal coordination and collaboration. The PCAs are:

- Cybersecurity and Information Assurance (CSIA)
- High Confidence Software and Systems (HCSS)
- High End Computing Infrastructure and Applications (HEC I&A)
- High End Computing Research and Development (HEC R&D)
- Human Computer Interaction and Information Management (HCI&IM)
- Large Scale Networking (LSN)
- Social, Economic, and Workforce Implications of IT and IT Workforce Development (SEW)
- Software Design and Productivity (SDP)

In each of these R&D areas, agency program managers meet in an IWG or CG to exchange information and collaborate on research plans and activities such as implementing testbeds, workshops, and cooperative solicitations. Such activities enable agencies to coordinate and focus their R&D resources on important, shared problems with the common goals of making new discoveries and/or developing new technological solutions. For example, information technology (IT) testbeds provide structured environments, akin to laboratory workbenches, where researchers test hypotheses, perform measurements, and collaborate under conditions similar to real-world environments. For agencies, the economic and engineering benefits of sharing IT testbed environments can be substantial, including avoiding the expense of duplicate facilities. Additional benefits accrue from cultivating a vibrant scientific and intellectual enterprise in which researchers across various agencies, disciplines, and sectors share ideas and results, speeding the overall pace of innovation.

Since 2008, the NITRD Program has given focus to emerging science and technology priorities by forming interagency Senior Steering Groups (SSGs) to work collaboratively on developing effective R&D strategies for national-level IT challenges. Implementing such R&D strategies may require multidisciplinary, multiagency, and multi-sector efforts and modifications to existing Federal R&D programs and policies. Thus, SSGs offer a means of cross-agency collaboration for senior-level individuals who have the authority to affect or shape the R&D directions of their organizations. The program focus areas coordinated by SSGs include:

- Big Data Research and Development (BD)

- Cyber Physical Systems Research and Development (CPS)

- Cybersecurity and Information Assurance Research and Development (CSIA R&D)

- Health Information Technology Research and Development (HITRD)

- Wireless Spectrum Research and Development (WSRD)

Additionally, the NITRD Program coordinates a group of science agency Chief Information Officers (CIOs) and/or their advanced technology specialists in a Community of Practice (CoP) with the goal of enhancing collaboration and accelerating agencies' adoption of advanced IT capabilities developed by government-sponsored IT research. The CoP is:

- Faster Administration of Science and Technology Education and Research (FASTER)

Overall NITRD Program coordination is carried out by the Subcommittee on Networking and Information Technology Research and Development, under the aegis of the Committee on Technology (CoT) of the National Science and Technology Council (NSTC). The NITRD Subcommittee convenes three times a year and the IWGs, CGs, CoP, and SSGs each meet approximately 12 times annually. The NITRD National Coordination Office (NITRD/NCO) provides technical, administrative, and logistical support for the activities of the NITRD Program, including publication of the annual NITRD Supplement to the President's Budget.

For further information about the NITRD Program, please see the NITRD website: http://www.nitrd.gov.

About the NITRD Supplement to the President's Budget

The annual Supplement to the President's Budget for the NITRD Program provides a technical summary of the research activities planned and coordinated through NITRD in a given Federal budget cycle, as required by law. The details are organized by PCA and presented using a common format:

- Listing of the NITRD member agencies and participating agencies active in the PCA

- Definition of the research covered in the PCA

- Strategic priorities in the PCA for the forthcoming fiscal year

- Budget highlights – agencies' key R&D programs and topical emphases in the PCA for the forthcoming year

- Interagency coordination – current and planned activities in which multiple agencies are collaborating

- Ongoing core activities of each agency in the PCA

The NITRD Supplement includes an annual budget table and budget analysis section, organized by PCA and by agency, to facilitate budgetary and programmatic comparisons from year to year.

In addition, the NITRD Supplement provides brief summaries of the interagency program focus areas coordinated under the NITRD Program's CoP and SSGs, including each group's strategic priorities and current and planned coordination activities for the forthcoming year.

The President's FY 2015 budget request for the NITRD Program is $3.8 billion and the 2014 NITRD budget estimates totaled $3.9 billion. Details of the budget are presented in the table on pages 8-9 and discussed in the budget analysis section.

The following illustration shows the percentages of the FY 2015 budget requests by PCA.

FY 2015 Budget Requests by PCA

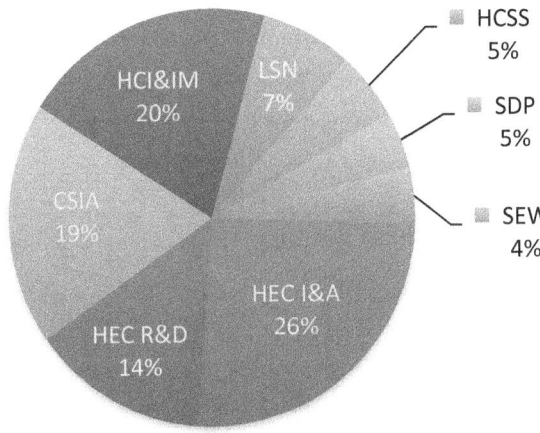

The following illustration shows the percentages of the FY 2015 budget requests by agency.

FY 2015 Budget Requests by Agency

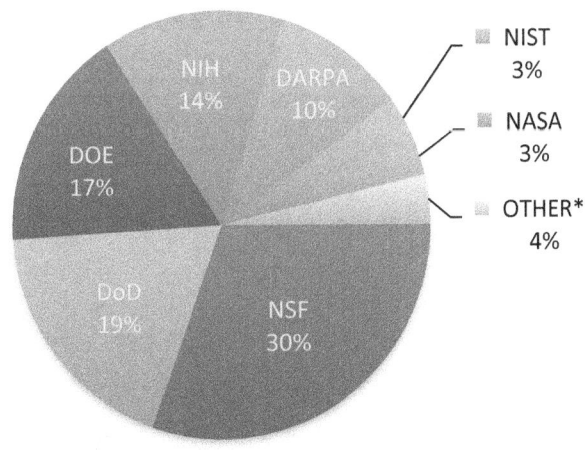

*Includes AHRQ, DHS, EPA, NARA, and NOAA.

The following illustration shows budget trends by PCA since FY 2000.[4]

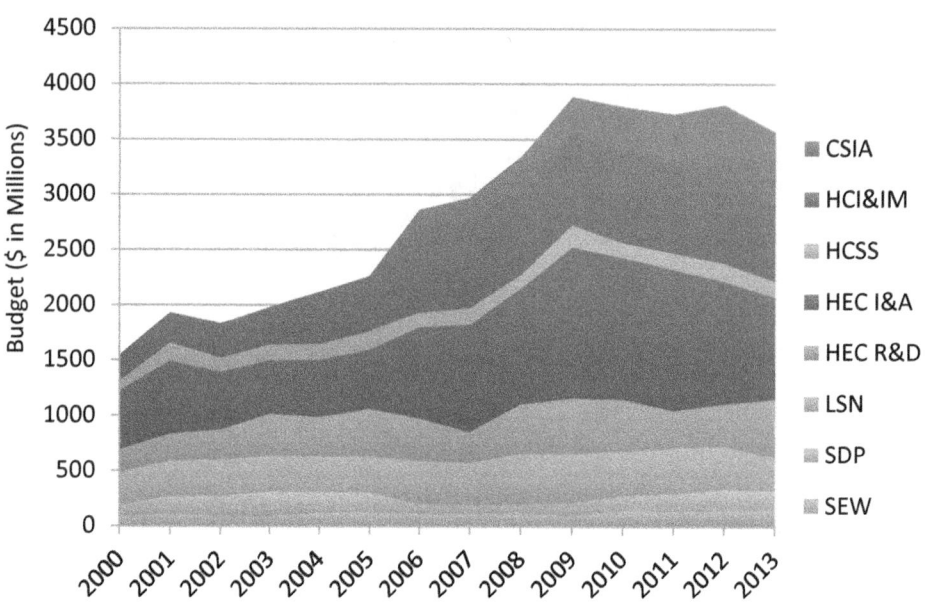

The following illustration shows budget trends by agency since FY 2000.[5]

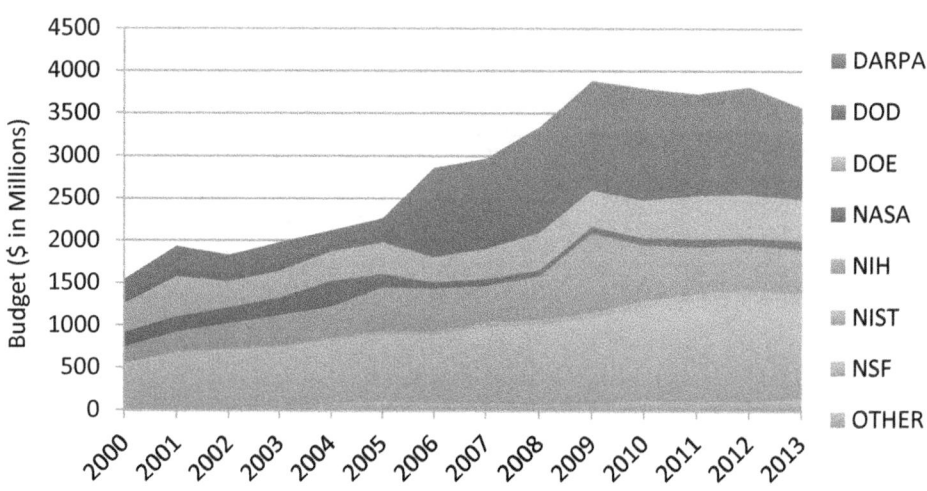

DOD includes OSD, NSA, and DoD Service research organizations. DOE includes DOE/NNSA, DOE/OE, and DOE/SC. OTHER includes AHRQ, DHS, EPA, NARA, and NOAA.

---

[4] The budget trends illustrations use budget estimates for FY 2000 - FY 2009 and budget actuals for FY 2010 and beyond.
[5] Same as footnote 4.

Agency NITRD Budgets by Program Component Area

Key: FY 2013 Budget Actuals, *FY 2014 Budget Estimates*, and **FY 2015 Budget Requests**
(Dollars in Millions)

Agency/ Program Component Area		Cybersecurity & Information Assurance (CSIA)	High Confidence Software & Systems (HCSS)	High End Computing Infrastructure & Applications (HEC I&A)	High End Computing Research & Development (HEC R&D)	Human Computer Interaction & Information Management (HCI&IM)	Large Scale Networking (LSN)	Social, Economic, & Workforce Implications of IT (SEW)	Software Design & Productivity (SDP)	Total[6]
NSF	FY 2013 Actual	97.9	87.4	235.6	112.2	284.8	119.0	112.6	83.7	1,133.1
	FY 2014 Estimate	*106.6*	*91.4*	*222.8*	*122.3*	*283.1*	*127.9*	*118.0*	*87.5*	*1,159.7*
	FY 2015 Request	**102.5**	**91.0**	**215.5**	**128.8**	**284.5**	**126.2**	**122.4**	**86.7**	**1,157.6**
DoD[7,8]		174.6	13.2	80.7	248.3	72.3	109.0	0.1	17.9	716.2
		192.1	*62.7*	*89.8*	*261.4*	*101.5*	*80.5*	*0.1*	*14.6*	*802.8*
		168.4	**39.3**	**81.1**	**212.5**	**131.5**	**62.7**		**8.6**	**704.2**
DOE[9]		32.6	2.5	307.5	80.1		43.4	6.0		472.1
		36.7	*7.5*	*343.2*	*107.4*		*71.2*			*566.0*
		30.0	**15.0**	**365.6**	**131.2**		**72.1**	**6.2**		**620.1**
NIH			20.0	189.0	17.0	214.0	3.0	23.0	56.0	522.0
			20.0	*195.0*	*17.0*	*220.0*	*3.0*	*24.0*	*57.0*	*536.0*
			20.0	**195.0**	**17.0**	**220.0**	**3.0**	**24.0**	**57.0**	**536.0**
DARPA		223.0				57.8	64.0	15.6		360.4
		293.5	*4.5*			*40.5*	*91.2*	*7.5*		*437.2*
		286.6	**9.0**			**27.7**	**70.3**			**393.5**
NIST[10]		49.7	8.7	15.3	5.6	11.5	6.8	0.4	4.3	102.2
		59.7	*11.5*	*16.0*	*5.6*	*11.5*	*6.8*	*4.4*	*4.4*	*119.8*
		59.7	**19.0**	**16.0**	**5.6**	**11.5**	**6.8**	**4.4**	**4.4**	**127.2**
NASA			17.2	62.7	0.4	17.0	1.0		9.6	107.9
			13.1	*73.2*	*0.6*	*17.0*	*1.0*		*10.8*	*115.7*
			12.4	**67.3**	**1.0**	**17.0**	**1.0**		**10.5**	**109.2**
DHS		75.3				3.2		4.0		82.5
		77.8				*10.0*		*3.8*		*91.6*
		67.5				**7.2**		**4.4**		**79.1**
NOAA				18.1	0.2	0.5	2.7		0.7	22.2
				21.4	*0.2*	*0.5*	*3.3*		*0.7*	*26.1*
				24.7	**0.2**	**0.5**	**3.3**		**0.7**	**29.4**
AHRQ						25.1	0.5			25.6
						29.1	*0.5*			*29.6*
						23.0	**0.5**			**23.5**
DOE/ NNSA[10]				9.0	5.0				3.0	17.0
				9.0	*5.0*				*3.0*	*17.0*
				8.9	**7.8**				**2.7**	**19.4**

[6] Totals may not sum correctly due to rounding.

[7] DoD budget includes funding for OSD, NSA, and the DoD Service research organizations. DoD Service research organizations include: Air Force Research Laboratory (AFRL), including the Air Force Office of Scientific Research (AFOSR); Army Research Laboratory (ARL), including the Army Research Office (ARO); Naval Research Laboratory (NRL); and Office of Naval Research (ONR). The Communications-Electronics Research, Development, and Engineering Center (CERDEC), Defense Research and Engineering Network (DREN), and High Performance Computing Modernization Program (HPCMP) are under Army. Although DARPA, NSA, and OSD research organizations are under DoD, they are independent of the research organizations of the DoD Services (Air Force, Army, and Navy).

[8] Data have been updated in the DoD/OSD lines in each of the reporting years, and differ from similar data presented in the Budget of the U.S. Government 2015.

[9] DOE budget includes funding from DOE's Office of Science (SC), Office of Electricity Delivery and Energy Reliability (OE), Energy Efficiency and Renewable Energy (EERE), and Energy Transformation Acceleration Fund.

[10] Data have been updated in the NIST and DOE/NNSA lines for the FY 2015 reporting year, and differ from similar data presented in the Budget of the U.S. Government 2015.

Agency/ Program Component Area		Cybersecurity & Information Assurance (CSIA)	High Confidence Software & Systems (HCSS)	High End Computing Infrastructure & Applications (HEC I&A)	High End Computing Research & Development (HEC R&D)	Human Computer Interaction & Information Management (HCI&IM)	Large Scale Networking (LSN)	Social, Economic, & Workforce Implications of IT (SEW)	Software Design & Productivity (SDP)	Total[6]
EPA	FY 2013 Actual				3.2	3.0				6.2
	FY 2014 Estimate				3.3	3.0				6.3
	FY 2015 Request				3.3	3.0				6.3
DOT[11]			1.5							1.5
			1.5							1.5
NARA						0.2				0.2
						0.2				0.2
						0.2				0.2
Total FY 2013 Actuals[6]		653.0	149.1	917.9	529.8	695.6	300.9	149.1	172.2	3,567.6
Total FY 2014 Estimates[6]		766.6	212.3	970.3	563.3	767.1	301.6	153.3	174.9	3,909.4
Total FY 2015 Requests[6]		714.7	207.2	974.1	535.0	768.5	275.6	164.1	167.9	3,807.2

NITRD Program Budget Analysis

Fiscal Year Overview for 2014-2015

In the following analysis of the NITRD Program, the President's FY 2015 request is compared with FY 2014 estimated spending. Changes in NITRD Program budgets reported in the budget analysis reflect revisions to program budgets due to evolving priorities, as well as Congressional actions and appropriations.

Summary

The President's 2015 budget request for the NITRD Program is $3.8 billion, a decrease of $100 million, approximately 2.6 percent less than the $3.9 billion 2014 estimate. The overall change is due to both increases and decreases in individual agency NITRD budgets, which are described below.

NITRD Program Budget Analysis by Agency

This section describes changes greater than $10 million between 2014 estimated spending and 2015 requests. Budget numbers in these descriptions are rounded from initial agency numbers with three decimals to the nearest tenth.

DoD

Comparison of 2014 estimate ($802.8 million) and 2015 request ($704.2 million): The $98.6 million decrease is primarily due to a decrease of $23.7 million in CSIA, $23.4 million in HCSS, $48.9 million in HEC R&D, and $17.8 million in LSN, with smaller decreases in other PCAs, partially offset by an increase of $30.0 million in HCI&IM.

DOE

Comparison of 2014 estimate ($566.0 million) and 2015 request ($620.1 million): The $54.1 million increase is primarily due to a $22.4 million increase in DOE/SC funding in HEC I&A for preparations for the next upgrades at the DOE's Leadership Computing Facilities and $23.8 million in HEC R&D for exascale and data-intensive science-related research, with smaller increases and decreases in other PCAs.

DARPA

Comparison of 2014 estimate ($437.2 million) and 2015 request ($393.5 million): The decrease of $43.7 million is primarily due to decreases of $12.8 million in HEC R&D for completion of the META program and $20.9 million in

---

[11] DOT budget is included to reflect funding for transportation initiatives beginning in FY 2014.

HCI&IM for completion of the Broad Operational Language Translation program, with smaller decreases and increases in other PCAs.

DHS

Comparison of 2014 estimate ($91.6 million) and 2015 request ($79.1 million): The $12.5 million decrease results primarily from a $10.3 million decrease in CSIA as a result of an overall reduction in the DHS Science and Technology Directorate (S&T) top line budget request for Research, Development, and Innovation (RD&I). This impacted all program areas within DHS S&T.

NITRD Program Budget Analysis by PCA

Using the information presented above, this section provides an analysis of the NITRD Program budget by PCA, summarizing the more substantial differences between 2014 estimated spending and 2015 requests. The changes are described below.

CSIA

Comparison of 2014 estimate ($766.6 million) and 2015 request ($714.7 million): The $51.9 million decrease is largely due to decreases of $23.7 million at DoD and $10.3 million at DHS, with smaller decreases at other agencies.

HEC R&D

Comparison of 2014 estimate ($563.3 million) and 2015 request ($535.0 million): The $28.3 million decrease is largely due to decreases of $48.9 million at DoD and $12.8 million at DARPA, partially offset by a $23.8 million increase at DOE and smaller increases at other agencies.

LSN

Comparison of 2014 estimate ($301.6 million) and 2015 request ($275.6 million): The $26.0 million decrease is largely due to a decrease of $17.8 million at DoD and $7.5 million at DARPA, with smaller decreases and increases at other agencies.

SEW

Comparison of 2014 estimate ($153.3 million) and 2015 request ($164.1 million): The $10.8 million increase is largely due to an increase of $6.2 million at DOE, with smaller increases and decreases at other agencies.

Budget Request by Program Component Area

Cyber Security and Information Assurance (CSIA)

**NITRD Agencies: AFOSR, AFRL, ARL, ARO, DARPA, DHS, DoD (CERDEC), DOE/OE, NIST, NSA, NSF, ONR, and OSD
Other Participants: DOT, IARPA, NRC, ODNI, and Treasury**

CSIA focuses on research and development to detect, prevent, resist, respond to, and recover from actions that compromise or threaten to compromise the availability, integrity, or confidentiality of computer- and network-based systems. These systems provide the IT foundation in every sector of the economy, including critical infrastructures such as power grids, financial systems, and air-traffic-control networks. These systems also support national defense, homeland security, and other Federal missions. Broad areas of emphasis include Internet and network security; security of information and computer-based systems; approaches to achieving hardware and software security; testing and assessment of computer-based systems security; reconstitution of computer-based systems and data; and resilience against cyber-attacks on computer-based systems that monitor, protect, and control critical infrastructure.

President's FY 2015 Request

Strategic Priorities Underlying This Request

In December 2011, the White House Office of Science and Technology Policy released *Trustworthy Cyberspace: Strategic Plan for the Federal Cybersecurity Research and Development Program*—a framework for a set of coordinated Federal strategic priorities and objectives for cybersecurity research. The Strategic Plan continues to define Federal research priorities in cybersecurity into FY 2015, reaffirmed by the OMB-OSTP Memorandum on Science and Technology Priorities for the FY 2015 Budget.[12] The Strategic Plan defines four areas for prioritizing research and development activities:

- **Inducing Change** – Utilizing game-changing themes to direct efforts toward understanding the underlying root causes of known threats with the goal of disrupting the status quo; the research themes include Moving Target, Tailored Trustworthy Spaces, Designed-In Security, and Cyber Economic Incentives

- **Developing Scientific Foundations** – Developing an organized, cohesive scientific foundation to the body of knowledge that informs the field of cybersecurity through adoption of a systematic, rigorous, and disciplined scientific approach

- **Maximizing Research Impact** – Catalyzing integration across the research themes, cooperation between governmental and private-sector communities, collaboration across international borders, and strengthened linkages to other national priorities, such as health IT and Smart Grid

- **Accelerating Transition to Practice** – Focusing efforts to ensure adoption and implementation of the new technologies and strategies that emerge from research and activities to build a scientific foundation so as to create measurable improvements in the cybersecurity landscape

In addition to the Strategic Plan, DoD agencies prioritize research investments to advance their cyber-supported warfighting capabilities:

- **Assuring the Mission** – Developing technologies to be aware of missions and threats, compute optimal assurance solutions, and implement protection as needed via mission agility or infrastructure reinforcement

---

[12] OMB-OSTP Memorandum on Science and Technology Priorities for the FY 2015 Budget (M-13-16), July 26, 2013: http://www.whitehouse.gov/sites/default/files/microsites/ostp/fy_15_memo_m-13-16.pdf

Highlights of Request

To address these strategic priorities, the CSIA agencies report the following topical areas as highlights of their planned R&D investments for FY 2015. Agencies are listed in alphabetical order:

- **Inducing change**
  - **Tailored Trustworthy Spaces theme**: Enable flexible, adaptive, distributed trust environments that can support functional and policy requirements arising from a wide spectrum of user activities in the face of an evolving range of threats.
    - Cyber physical systems security – DHS, NIST, and NSF
    - Trusted foundation for defensive cyberspace operations – AFRL, ARL, ARO, CERDEC, ONR, and OSD
    - High assurance security architectures – AFRL, DARPA, NIST, NSA, ONR, and OSD
    - IT Security Automation/Continuous Monitoring/Security Content Automation Protocol Program – DHS, NIST, and NSA
    - Security for cloud-based systems – AFOSR, AFRL, DARPA, DHS, NIST, and NSF
    - Secure wireless networking – ARL, ARO, CERDEC, DARPA, NSA, NSF, ONR, and OSD
    - Secure and Trustworthy Cyberspace (SaTC) Program – NSF
    - Digital Provenance and Hardware-Enabled Trust Programs – DHS
    - Security for Tactical Operations Relying on Methods for Enhancing Robustness (STORMER) – ARL
    - Cybersecurity for Energy Delivery Systems (CEDS) Program – DOE/OE
  - **Moving Target theme**: Develop capabilities to create, analyze, evaluate, and deploy mechanisms and strategies that are diverse and that continually shift and change over time to increase complexity and the cost for attackers, limit the exposure of vulnerabilities and malicious opportunities, and increase system resiliency.
    - Embedded System Resiliency and Agility – AFRL
    - Configuration-Based Moving Target Defense – AFRL
    - Cyber Maneuver – ARL
    - Adaptive Cyber Defense MURI – ARL
    - Cyber Agility Program – AFRL
    - Secure and Trustworthy Cyberspace (SaTC) Program – NSF
    - Moving Target Defense Program – DHS
    - Proactive and Reactive Adaptive Systems – NSA
    - Security Automation and Vulnerability Management – NIST
    - Trust Management in Service Oriented Architectures – ONR
    - Robust Autonomic Computing System – ONR
    - Information Security Automation Program (ISAP) – DHS, NIST, and NSA
    - Active Repositioning in Cyberspace for Synchronized Evasion (ARCSYNE) – AFRL
    - Morphing Network Assets to Restrict Adversarial Reconnaissance (Morphinator) – ARL, ARO, and CERDEC

- Defensive Enhancements for Information Assurance Technologies (DEFIANT) – ARL, ARO, and CERDEC
- Clean-slate design of Resilient, Adaptive, Secure Hosts (CRASH) and Mission-Oriented Resilient Clouds (MRC) Programs – AFRL, DARPA
- Cybersecurity for Energy Delivery Systems (CEDS) Program – DOE/OE
- Autonomic Cyber Agility – OSD

- o **Cyber Economic Incentives theme**: Develop effective market-based, legal, regulatory, or institutional incentives to make cybersecurity ubiquitous, including incentives affecting individuals and organizations.
  - Secure and Trustworthy Cyberspace (SaTC) Program – NSF
  - Cyber Economics Incentives Research Program – DHS
  - Cybersecurity for Energy Delivery Systems (CEDS) Program – DOE/OE

- o **Designed-in Security theme**: Develop capabilities to design and evolve high-assurance, software-intensive systems predictably and reliably while effectively managing risk, cost, schedule, quality, and complexity. Create tools and environments that enable the simultaneous development of cyber-secure systems and the associated assurance evidence necessary to prove the system's resistance to vulnerabilities, flaws, and attacks.
  - Survivable Systems Engineering – OSD
  - Trusted Computing – AFRL, NSA, and OSD
  - Software Development Environment for Secure System Software and Applications – ONR
  - Roots of Trust – AFRL, NIST, and NSA
  - Secure and Trustworthy Cyberspace (SaTC) Program – NSF
  - Software Assurance Toolkit (SWAT) – ARL
  - Static Tool Analysis Modernization Project (STAMP) – DHS
  - Software Assurance Metrics And Tool Evaluation (SAMATE) – DHS and NIST
  - Automated Program Analysis for Cybersecurity (APAC) – DARPA
  - High-Assurance Cyber Military Systems (HACMS) – DARPA
  - Cybersecurity for Energy Delivery Systems (CEDS) Program – DOE/OE
  - PROgramming Computation on EncryptEd Data (PROCEED) – AFRL and DARPA

- **Assuring the Mission**: Provide the ability to avoid, fight through, survive, and recover from advanced cyber threats.
  - o Cyber Survivability and Recovery II – AFRL
  - o Mission Awareness for Mission Assurance – AFRL
  - o Cyber-Based Mission Assurance on Trust-Enhanced Hardware (CMATH) – AFRL
  - o Proactive Cyber-Physical System Defense – ONR
  - o Assuring Effective Missions – OSD

- **Developing Scientific Foundations**
  - ○ **Science of Security**: In anticipation of the challenges in securing the cyber systems of the future, the Federal research in the areas of science of security aims to develop an organized, scientific foundation that informs the cybersecurity domain, by organizing disparate areas of knowledge, enabling discovery of universal laws, and by applying the rigor of the scientific method.
    - ▪ Cyber Collaborative Research Alliance (Cyber CRA) – ARL
    - ▪ Science for Cybersecurity (S4C) – ARL and ARO
    - ▪ Science of Security MURI – AFOSR
    - ▪ Trust and Suspicion Basic Research Initiative – AFOSR
    - ▪ Cyber measurement and experimentation – OSD
    - ▪ Cybersecurity for Energy Delivery Systems (CEDS) Program – DOE/OE
    - ▪ Secure and Trustworthy Cyberspace (SaTC) Program – NSF
  - ○ **Cross-cutting foundations**:
    - ▪ Cryptography – DARPA, NIST, NSA, NSF, and ONR
    - ▪ Models, standards, testing, and metrics – ARL, ARO, DHS, DOE/OE, NIST, NSF, and OSD
    - ▪ Foundations of Trust – AFRL, ARL, ARO, CERDEC, DARPA, DOE/OE, NIST, NSA, NSF, ONR, and OSD
    - ▪ Security Management and Assurance Standards – NIST
    - ▪ Quantum information science and technology – AFRL, DOE/OE, IARPA, NIST, and ONR
- **Maximizing Research Impact**
  - ○ **Supporting national priorities**: The cybersecurity research themes provide a framework for addressing the cybersecurity R&D requirements associated with national priorities in, for example, the healthcare, energy, financial services, and defense sectors.
    - ▪ National Critical Infrastructure Security and Resilience R&D Plan (Presidential Policy Directive 21, "Critical Infrastructure Security and Resilience") – DHS, DOE/OE
    - ▪ Standards Framework for Critical Infrastructure Protection (Executive Order 13636, "Improving Critical Infrastructure Cybersecurity") – NIST
    - ▪ Cybersecurity Education and Workforce Development – DHS, NIST, NSF
    - ▪ National Strategy for Trusted Identities in Cyberspace (NSTIC) – NIST
    - ▪ Health IT Security Program – NIST
    - ▪ Trustworthy Cyber Infrastructure for the Power Grid (TCIPG) – DHS and DOE/OE
    - ▪ Smart Grid Interoperability Panel (SGIP) - Smart Grid Cybersecurity Committee (SGCC) – DOE/OE and NIST
    - ▪ Journal of Sensitive Cybersecurity Research and Engineering (JSCoRE) – ODNI
- **Accelerating Transition to Practice**
  - ○ **Technology discovery, evaluation, transition, adoption, and commercialization**: Explicit, coordinated processes that transition the fruits of research into practice to achieve significant and long-lasting impact.

- ▪ Cyber Security Research Infrastructure (Experimental Research Test Bed (DETER), Research Data Repository (PREDICT), Software Assurance Market Place (SWAMP) – DHS

- ▪ Center for Advanced Communications – NIST

- ▪ DoD Cyber Transition to Practice Initiative – OSD

- ▪ Testbeds and infrastructure for R&D – DARPA, DHS, NSF, and OSD

- ▪ Transition to Practice Program – DHS

- ▪ Information Technology Security Entrepreneurs' Forum (ITSEF) – DHS

- ▪ Secure and Trustworthy Cyberspace (SaTC) Program – NSF

- ▪ Small Business Innovative Research (SBIR) Conferences – DHS and DoD

- ▪ National Cybersecurity Center of Excellence (NCCoE) – NIST

- ▪ Cybersecurity for Energy Delivery Systems (CEDS) Program – DOE/OE

- ▪ Cyber Grand Challenge (CGC) – DARPA

Planning and Coordination Supporting Request

The CSIA agencies engage in a variety of cooperative efforts – from implementing multiagency testbeds essential for experimentation with new technologies at realistic scales, to collaborative deployment of prototypes, to common standards. The following is a representative summary of current multiagency collaborations:

- **Co-funding**: Trustworthy Cyber Infrastructure for the Power Grid (TCIPG) – DHS and DOE/OE; Defense Technology Experimental Research (DETER) testbed – DHS and NSF; National Centers of Academic Excellence in Information Assurance Education and Research – DHS and NSA

- **Workshops**: Cybersecurity Applications and Technology Conference for Homeland Security – DHS; DoD Small Business Innovation Research (SBIR) Conference – DHS and OSD; Annual IT Security Automation Conference – DHS, NIST, and NSA; National Initiative for Cybersecurity Education Annual Workshop – DHS, NIST, NSA, NSF, and OSD; Cloud Forums – DHS, GSA, and NIST; Mobile Security Forum – NIST and NSA; IT Security Entrepreneur Forum, Innovation Summit, SINET Showcase, Transition To Practice Showcase – DHS; Trustworthy Cyber Infrastructure for the Power Grid (TCIPG) Industry Workshop – DHS and DOE/OE; Workshops on Incorporating Security Concepts in Undergraduate Computer Science Curriculum – NSF; International Conference on Software Security and Reliability – NIST; Computational Cybersecurity in Compromised Environments (C3E) Workshops – ODNI

- **Collaborative deployment**: DNS security (DNSSEC) and routing security – AFRL, DHS, and NIST; The National Vulnerability Database – DHS and NIST; U.S. Government Configuration Baseline (USGCB) – NIST and NSA

- **Interagency cooperation**: Ongoing information exchanges in support of developing a national cybersecurity R&D agenda – All CSIA agencies

- **Technical standards**: Developing, maintaining, and coordinating validation programs for cryptographic standards – NIST and NSA; participation in Internet Engineering Task Force (IETF) security groups to develop standard representations and corresponding reference implementations of security-relevant data – DHS, NIST, NSA, and OSD; Smart Grid Interoperability Panel (SGIP) - Smart Grid Cybersecurity Committee (SGCC) – DOE/OE and NIST

- **Testbeds**: Continued joint development of research testbeds, such as DETER, Protected Repository for the Defense of Infrastructure Against Cyber Threats (PREDICT), Distributed Environment for Critical Infrastructure Decision-making Exercises (DECIDE), Wisconsin Advanced Internet Laboratory (WAIL), Mobile Networks Testbed Emulation – ARL, ARO, CERDEC, DHS, DOE/OE, NSF, ONR, and Treasury

- **DoD Cyber Science and Technology Priority Steering Council (Cyber PSC)**: Oversight and coordination of all defensive cyber S&T programs – OSD and DoD Service research organizations

- **Technical Cooperation Program Communications, Command, Control and Intelligence (C3I) Group**: Information assurance and defensive information warfare – AFRL, ARL, ARO, CERDEC, NSA, ONR, and OSD

- **International collaboration**: NSF and the U.S.-Israel Binational Science Foundation joint program; Network and Information Sciences International Technology Alliance (U.S. Army-United Kingdom collaborative program on secure data sharing and research collaboration among coalition partners); DHS International Engagements and co-funding activities with Australia, Canada, Germany, Israel, Netherlands, Sweden, United Kingdom, European Union, Japan

- **Cyber education**: Centers of Academic Excellence – NSA; CyberCorps: Scholarship for Service – NSF; National Initiative for Cybersecurity Education (NICE) – DHS, NIST, NSA, NSF, ODNI, and OSD; Cybersecurity Competitions – DHS

Additional 2014 and 2015 Activities by Agency

The following list provides a summary of individual agencies' ongoing programmatic interests for 2014 and 2015 under the CSIA PCA:

- **AFRL**: Secure systems foundations; foundations for trusted architectures; cyber agility (configuration-based moving target defense, polymorphic machines, polymorphic enclaves, IP hopping); cyber survivability and recovery (mission survival/recovery in the cloud, survive with mission assurance, recover with immunity), mission aware cyber command and control (integration of Command and Control of Cyber Assets for Mission Assurance [C2 CAMA], Assured Dynamic Configuration [ADC], User-Defined Operational Picture [UDOP]); mission-centric cyber assurance (mission assurance in the cloud, data hiding and analysis, threat abatement, assured resources); Assured by Design (science of mission assurance, domain modification, engineering assured systems)

- **ARL, ARO, and CERDEC**: Mobile security (tactical edge solutions for the dismounted warfighter); cyber maneuver (network and platform agility for mission assurance, cyber deception); cyber frameworks (capabilities built on open, sustainable and well-defined specifications and frameworks for defensive and offensive operations); software defined radio protection (waveform and protocol IDS, RF jamming protection, modularized radio security architecture); software assurance; trust research (trust management for optimal network performance, models and analytical tools for social-media-based data sensing and processing); intrusion detection (automated signature generation and anomaly detection); dynamic continuous risk monitoring and risk scoring; trusted social computing; hardware assurance; cyber SA

- **DARPA**: Information Assurance and Survivability (core computing and networking technologies to protect DoD's information, information infrastructure, and mission-critical information systems; tools and methods to uncover hidden malicious functionality; algorithms for detecting anomalous and threat-related behaviors; more effective user identification and authentication techniques; methods to enable assured and trustworthy Internet communications and computation; and cost-effective security and survivability solutions)

- **DHS**: Cyber transition and outreach (Transition to Practice [TTP], cybersecurity outreach); network and system security integration (cybersecurity for law enforcement, data privacy and identity management, disrupting cyber threats and inducing change, improving foundational elements of cybersecurity, leap ahead technologies); trustworthy cyberinfrastructure (internet measurement and attack modeling, process control system security, secure protocols); cybersecurity user protection and education (cybersecurity competitions, cybersecurity forensics, data privacy technologies, identity management)

- **DOE/OE**: Continue to align research activities with the DOE-facilitated, energy sector-led *Roadmap to Achieve Energy Delivery Systems Cybersecurity*, updated in 2011, strategic framework and vision that by 2020, resilient energy delivery systems are designed, installed, operated, and maintained to survive a cyber-incident while sustaining critical functions. Collaborate with all energy sector stakeholders including national laboratories, academia, technology vendors, energy asset owners, and Federal partners

- **IARPA**: Securely Taking on New Executable Software of Uncertain Provenance (STONESOUP); SPAR Program (parsimonious information sharing: minimizing collateral information that must be shared in order to efficiently share a desired piece of information); quantum computer science; trusted integrated circuits; Tools for Recognizing Useful Signals of Trustworthiness (TRUST) Program

- **NIST**: Foundations (risk management, identity management, key management, security automation, vulnerability management, cryptography); security overlays (healthcare, Smart Grid, cyber-physical systems, public safety networks, trusted identities); security and mobility; continuous monitoring; biometrics; Security Content Automation Protocol; security for cloud computing; security for electronic voting; usable security; and supply chain risk management; robust and interoperable healthcare enterprise (test methods and standards, seamless interoperability of Electronic Health Records (EHRs), methods to test terminologies/vocabularies, test methods for medical device interoperability, interoperability test-bed); Big Data Initiative (Big Data framework, standards, interoperability, portability, reusability, extendibility, technology roadmap); participation in standards development organizations; techniques for measuring and managing security; metrology infrastructure for modeling and simulation; National Initiative for Cybersecurity Education (NICE)

- **NSA**: Trusted computing (high assurance security architectures enabled by virtualization, improved enterprise protection through strong software measurement and reporting); mobility (secure enterprise infrastructure required for secure mobility, improved physical protection of mobile assets, location sensitive access control, cost-effective protection of air interface, integrating data from different sensors (host, LAN, gateway), non-signature based detection); systems behavior

- **NSF**: Secure and Trustworthy Cyberspace (SaTC) program: a joint program by the NSF Directorates of Computer and Information Science and Engineering (CISE), Mathematical and Physical Sciences (MPS), Social, Behavioral and Economic Sciences (SBE), Education and Human Resources (EHR), and Engineering (ENG)

- **ONR**: Cyber information infrastructure (resilient autonomic computing, dynamically reconfigurable computing systems, data science, data security, software science, tactical cloud, SOA and beyond, quantum computing, bio / analog computing, novel network architectures and protocols; electronics; apertures; radios; tactical networks; interactive devices); foundations of discovery and search (data representation and models; automated analysis and understanding of data, signal, activity, and intent; machine learning and reasoning; self-aware/mission-aware/self-reconfigurable dynamic networked sensing; distributed control); rapid and accurate decision making (automated cyber/ISR/C2/CS information sharing, integration, understanding and management; automated courses of action generation; automated decision tools that recommend optimized options in mission context; dynamic battle-space SA at cyber speed); proactive cyber-physical system defense (synergistic integration of network sensing, reasoning and control for intelligence-driven information assurance and cyber-physical system defense via automation and machine situational awareness)

- **OSD**: Cyber Applied Research Program (emphasis on development of new security frameworks and methods); Cyber Advanced Technology Development Program (integrate and mature Service Laboratory and NSA research for new joint capabilities, build on results of matured applied research to develop technology for potential transition); assuring effective missions (cyber mission control, effects at scale); cyber agility (autonomic cyber agility, cyber maneuver); cyber resilience (resilient architectures, resilient algorithms and protocols); foundations of trust (system-level trust, trustworthy components and mechanisms); modeling, simulation, and experimentation; embedded, mobile, and tactical; cyber security metrics; DoD Cyber Transition to Practice; and SBIR workshop to facilitate networking with small businesses

High Confidence Software and Systems (HCSS)

NITRD Agencies: DARPA, DHS, DoD Service Research Organizations, NASA, NIH, NIST, NSA, NSF, and OSD
Other Participants: DOT, FAA, FDA, FHWA, NRC, and USDA

HCSS R&D supports development of scientific foundations and innovative and enabling software and hardware technologies for the engineering, verification and validation, assurance, standardization, and certification of complex, networked, distributed computing systems and cyber-physical (IT-enabled) systems (CPS). The goal is to enable seamless, fully synergistic integration of computational intelligence, communication, control, sensing, actuation, and adaptation with physical devices and information processes to routinely realize high-confidence, optimally performing systems that are essential for effectively operating life-, safety-, security-, and mission-critical applications. These systems must be capable of interacting correctly, safely, and securely with humans and the physical world in changing environments and unforeseen conditions. In many cases, they must be certifiably dependable. The vision is to realize dependable systems that are precise and highly efficient; respond quickly; work in dangerous or inaccessible environments; provide large-scale, distributed coordination; augment human capabilities; and enhance societal quality of life. New science and technology are needed to build these systems with computing, communication, information, and control pervasively embedded at all levels, thus enabling entirely new generations of engineering designs that can enhance U.S. competitiveness across economic and industrial sectors.

President's FY 2015 Request

Strategic Priorities Underlying This Request

In recent years, the HCSS agencies have engaged in a sustained effort to foster a new multidisciplinary research agenda that will enable the United States to lead in the development of next-generation engineered systems that depend on ubiquitous cyber control and require very high levels of system assurance. Through a variety of ongoing activities, the HCSS effort is forging a nationwide community interested in the CPS research challenges faced in common across such economic sectors as medicine and healthcare, energy, transportation, manufacturing, and agriculture, and across such agency missions as national security, environmental protection, and space exploration. The HCSS agencies have set the following priorities for research coordination:

- **Science and technology for building cyber-physical systems**: Develop a new systems science providing unified foundations, models and tools, system capabilities, and architectures that enable innovation in highly dependable cyber-enabled engineered and natural systems; develop public domain, cyber-physical testbeds

- **Management of complex and autonomous systems**: Develop measurement and understanding for improved models of complex systems of systems, shared control and authority, levels of autonomy, human-system interactions, and new integrated analytical and decision-support tools; develop Engineered Resilient Systems (ERS); integrate computer and information-centric physical and engineered systems

- **Assurance technology**: Develop a sound scientific and technological basis, including formal methods and computational frameworks, for assured design, construction, analysis, evaluation, and implementation of reliable, robust, safe, secure, stable, and certifiably dependable systems regardless of size, scale, complexity, and heterogeneity; develop software and system-engineering tool capabilities to achieve application and problem domain-based assurance, and broadly embed these capabilities within the system engineering process; reduce the effort, time, and cost of assurance ("affordable" V&V/certification); provide a technology base of advanced-prototype implementations of high-confidence technologies to spur adoption; design and install resilient energy delivery systems capable of surviving a cyber-incident while sustaining critical functions; support development of regulations and guidance for assurance of safety and security

- **High-confidence real-time software and systems**: Pursue innovative design, development, and engineering approaches to ensure the dependability, safety, security, performance, and evolution of software-intensive, dynamic, networked control systems in life- and safety-critical infrastructure domains, including systems-of-systems environments; real-time embedded applications and systems software; component-based accelerated design and verifiable system integration; predictable, fault-tolerant, distributed software and systems; modeling of heterogeneous distributed systems using unified mathematical framework; develop safety assurance tools and techniques to build justifiable confidence in aerospace and national airspace systems; develop infrastructure for medical device integration and interoperability, patient modeling and simulation, and adaptive patient-specific algorithms

- **Translation into mission-oriented research**: Leverage multiagency research to move theory into practice, using challenges and competitions, for example, to solve problems in domains such as energy, cyber-physical ground and air transportation systems, and connected vehicle-to-infrastructure systems

- **CPS education**: Launch an initiative to integrate CPS theory and methodology into education and promote increased understanding of and interest in CPS through the development of new curricula at all levels that engages both the physical and cyber disciplines and fosters a new generation of U.S. experts

Highlights of the Request

The HCSS agencies report the following topical areas as highlights of their planned R&D investments for FY 2015. Agencies are listed in alphabetical order:

- **Cyber-physical systems**: Explore the fundamental scientific, engineering, and technological principles that underpin the integration of cyber and physical elements, making the "systems you can bet your life on" possible; continue support for research to enable physical, biological, and engineered systems whose operations are integrated, monitored, and/or controlled by a computational core and interact with the physical world, with components networked at every scale and computing deeply embedded in every physical component, possibly even in materials; real-time embedded, distributed systems and software; CEMMSS to model and simulate systems interdependent with the physical world and social systems; safety models and designs for cyber-physical medical systems, including interoperable ("plug-and-play") medical devices – DARPA, DoD Service research organizations, FDA, NASA, NIH, NIST, NSA, NSF, OSD, and VA

- **Complex systems**: Multiyear effort, including focus on software for tomorrow's complex systems such as CPS, to address challenges of interacting systems of systems, including human-system interactions, and investigate their non-linear interactions and aggregate or emergent phenomena to better predict system capabilities and decision-making about complex systems; develop new algorithms for functional analysis of real-time software, control effects of multicore memory access on CPS real-time behavior, and flexible and predictable control of multiple, semi-autonomous UAVs; joint capability technology demonstration of flexible mission-reprogramming, increased endurance, and increased autonomy – AFRL, FAA, NASA, NIH, NIST, NSF, and OSD

- **High-confidence systems and foundations of assured computing**: Formal methods and tools for modeling, designing, measuring, analyzing, evaluating, and predicting performance, correctness, efficiency, dependability, scalability, safety, security, and usability of complex, real-time, distributed, and mobile software and systems; high-assurance environments from COTs; high-assurance virtualization and measurement; architectures, components, composition, and configuration; engineering, analysis, and testing of software and hardware; architecture, tools, and competence for assurance certifiable safe systems; cost-effective V&V; verification techniques for separation assurance algorithms; safety cases, standards, and metrics; quantum information processing – AFOSR, AFRL, ARO, DARPA, FDA, NASA, NIH, NIST, NSA, NSF, ONR, and OSD

- **Information assurance requirements**: Methods and tools for constructing, analyzing security structures (management architectures and protocols, etc.); assurance technologies for cross-domain creation, editing, sharing of sensitive information in collaboration environments that span multiple security levels; cryptographic algorithms and engineering; assured compilation of cryptographic designs, specifications to platforms of interest - NSA and ONR; testing infrastructure for health IT standards, specifications, certification (with HHS); cross-enterprise document sharing in electronic health systems; standards and quality measurement systems for smart manufacturing, measurement science and standards for CPS engineering; build a testbed to help industry, university, and government collaborators develop an open standards platform to facilitate the simultaneous engineering of the physical and virtual components of manufacturing systems – NIH, NIST, and NSF

- **Aviation safety**: R&D in transformative V&V methods to rigorously assure the safety of aviation systems. This includes considerations for all classes of aircraft and anticipated future air traffic management capabilities; and develop and demonstrate innovative technologies in the design of architectures with advanced features, focusing on designing for high-confidence, standardization, and certification – AFRL, FAA, NASA, and OSD

- **Assurance of Flight-Critical Systems (AFCS)**: Provide appropriate airworthiness requirements for Unmanned Aircraft Systems (UAS) that help enable routine access to the national airspace system; enable assurance that new technologies envisioned for the Next Generation Air Transportation System (NextGen) are as safe as, or safer than, the current system and provide a cost-effective basis for assurance and certification of complex civil aviation systems; develop and analyze formal models of air traffic management systems for safety properties incorporating the effects of uncertainty – AFRL, FAA, and NASA

Planning and Coordination Supporting Request

To build multidisciplinary communities of interest both within and across sectors, the HCSS agencies have developed a busy annual schedule, which will continue through FY 2015, of workshops and other research meetings that bring a broad mix of stakeholders together. The HCSS workshops on high-confidence medical devices, for example, draws medical researchers, medical practitioners and caregivers, device developers and vendors, care facility administrators, academic computer scientists and engineers, and Federal Government regulators. These unique gatherings are forging wider understanding of critical issues and developing consensus around promising research directions in high-confidence CPS. Similarly, HCSS-sponsored workshops on transportation CPS are developing agreement on R&D needs that span multiple transportation sectors. In summary, the following are ongoing HCSS coordination activities:

- **National Research Workshop Series**: Academic, industry, and government stakeholder workshops to identify new R&D for building 21st century CPS for life-, safety-, and mission-critical applications; topics include:

  - **High Confidence Medical Device CPS** – "National Workshop on Research Frontiers in Medical Cyber-Physical Systems" – FDA, NIST, NSA, and NSF

  - **Future Energy CPS** – "National Workshop on Energy Cyber-Physical Systems" – NIST, NSA, and NSF

  - **High Confidence Transportation CPS**: "National Workshop on Transportation Cyber-Physical Systems" – AFRL, DOT, FAA, FDA, FHWA, NASA, NIST, NSA, and NSF

  - **CPS Week** – Annual High Confidence Networked Systems (HiCoNS) meeting – AFRL, DHS, NASA, NIST, NSA, and NSF

  - **Static Analysis Tools Exposition (SATE)**: Annual summit on software security for vendors, users, and academics – NIST, NSA, and NSF in collaboration with DHS

  - **CPS Education**: NSA, NSF, and ONR

- **Scholar In Residence Program** – FDA and NSF

- **Software Assurance Metrics and Tool Evaluation**: Annual workshop for users and developers to compare efficacy of techniques and tools; develop vulnerability taxonomies – DHS, NIST, and NSA

- **Safe and Secure Software and Systems Symposium (S5)**: Industry, academia, and government collaborate on improving the airworthiness and assurance certification process of future aerospace flight control systems with both incremental and revolutionary technological innovations in safety and security verification and validation (V&V) techniques that support maintaining cost and risk at acceptable levels – AFRL, NASA, NSA, and NSF

- **Annual HCSS Conference**: Showcasing of promising research to improve system confidence – FAA, NASA, NSA with NSF, ONR, and OSD

- **Software Assurance Forum**: Coordinate software certification initiatives and activities for Systems containing Software (ScS) – DHS, DoD Service research organizations, NIST, NSA, and OSD

- **Safety of flight-critical systems**: Workshops and technical discussion – AFRL, NASA, NSA, and NSF

- **Standards, software assurance metrics for Supervisory Control and Data Acquisition (SCADA), Industrial Control Systems (ICS)**: Collaborative development – NIST and others

- **Biomedical imagery**: Technical standards for change measurements in patient applications – FDA, NIH, and NIST

- **Cooperative proposal evaluation** – AFRL, DARPA, FAA, FDA, NASA, NIST, NRC, NSA, NSF, and OSD

- **FAA National Software and Airborne Electronic Hardware Standardization Conference** – FAA and NASA

- **6th NASA Formal Methods Symposium (NFM 2014)** – AFRL, FAA, FDA, NASA, NIST, NSF, and NSA

- **Exploratory Advanced Research (EAR) Program**: Connected Highway Vehicle System concepts, with human and hardware-in-the-loop, and adaptive hardware, structures, and pavements – DOT, FHWA, NIST, and NSF

- **National Robotics Initiative (NRI)**: Cross-cutting program to accelerate the development and use of robots that work beside, or cooperatively with, people – NASA, NIH, NSF, and USDA

Additional 2014 and 2015 Activities by Agency

The following list provides a summary of individual agencies' ongoing programmatic interests for 2014 and 2015 under the HCSS PCA:

- **AFRL**: Aviation safety and security R&D of improved system design methodologies (to include but not limited to model-based systems engineering) and enhanced V&V techniques supporting airworthiness certification of autonomous, flight-critical systems operating in a dynamic, system-of-systems environment. Develop innovative, usable, and more cost effective formalized mathematical frameworks to shift the burden of traditional test-based verification to early analysis and synthesized "correct-by-construction" systems. Shift the burden of offline analysis for machine intelligence and decision-making in complex, uncertain, and dynamic environments by increasing reliance on more run-time assurances. Develop methods to ensure reliability of human-machine communication and interaction through formal guarantees. Develop rigorous and verifiable architecture constructs for data-centric autonomous systems

- **DARPA**: Develop technologies to secure mission-critical embedded computing systems in ground vehicles and unmanned aerial vehicles. Use recent advances in program synthesis, formal verification techniques, and low-level and domain-specific programming languages to produce fully verified operating systems for embedded devices

- **FAA**: Improve and maintain methods for approving digital systems for aircraft and air traffic control (ATC) systems and prepare for the Next Generation Air Transportation System (NextGen) by conducting research in advanced digital (software-based and airborne electronic hardware [AEH]-based airborne systems) technology; keep abreast of and adapt to the rapid, frequent changes and increasing complexity in aircraft and ATC systems; understand and assess safe implementations in flight-essential and flight-critical systems (e.g., fly-by-wire flight controls, navigation and communication equipment, autopilots, and other aircraft and engine functions); and continue work on digital requirements for software-development techniques and tools, airborne electronic hardware design techniques and tools, onboard network security and integrity, and system considerations for complex digitally intensive systems

- **FDA**: Formal methods-based design (assured verification, device software and system safety modeling and certification, component composition, forensics analysis, engineering tool foundations); architecture, platform, middleware, resource management for interoperable medical devices (plug-and-play, vigilance and trending systems); infrastructure for medical-device integration, interoperation; patient modeling, simulation; adaptive patient-specific algorithms; and black box/data loggers and analysis

- **FHWA**: Continue to apply concepts from fundamental advances in cyber-physical science to develop a new transportation paradigm of connected highway and vehicle systems in support of broad mission goals, including making traffic deaths or serious injuries rare events, optimizing mobility so that personal travel and goods movement are easy and reliable within, between, and across modal systems, and reducing the energy and resources required for highway transportation in the U.S. Also enhance research, development, and technology for health monitoring of highway transportation structures and pavements to include control from the nano through micro to the macro scale to create true, fully functioning cyber-physical systems that will ensure a state of good repair for the Nation's roads and respond to both every day and extreme environmental changes

- **NASA**: Aviation safety R&D with emphasis on enabling technologies for design, V&V of flight-critical systems (argument-based safety assurance, autonomy and authority, integrated distributed systems, software-intensive systems); enabling assurance technologies for NextGen self-separation concepts; and determining appropriate airworthiness requirements for UAS to help enable routine access to the national airspace

- **NIH**: Translational research in biomedical technology to enhance development, testing, and implementation of diagnostics and therapeutics that require advanced CPS innovations; assurance in medical devices such as pulse oximeters and infusion pumps, cardio-exploratory monitors for neonates; telemedicine; computer-aided detection and diagnosis; computer-aided surgery and treatment; neural interface technologies such as cochlear implants, and brain-computer interfaces. Systematic exploration of the sources and variability introduced during tumor image acquisition and tumor size measurement, for the development of improved algorithms used in assessment of new therapies; and development of new data acquisition and analysis methods to aid in the determination of optimal ultrasound exposure settings to obtain the necessary diagnostic information by using the very lowest total energy for increased patient safety

- **NIST**: Computer forensics tool testing; National Software Reference Library (funded by DOJ/National Institute for Justice [NIJ]); National Vulnerability Database; Internet infrastructure protection (with DHS funding); seamless mobility; trustworthy information systems; information security automation, Security Content Automation Protocol (SCAP); combinatorial testing; next-generation access control; smart manufacturing; and automotive CPS

- **NRC**: Regulatory research to assure safety and security in cyber-physical systems (digital instrumentation and control systems) used in the nuclear energy sector

- **NSA**: High-assurance system design (correct-by-construction methods, model-driven development, programming languages) and analysis (concolic execution, multi-tool analysis, separation/matching logic, static/dynamic analysis), with focus on usability; assured implementation, execution of critical platform components and functionality; and assured cryptographic implementations (software and hardware); domain-specific workbench developments (cryptography, guards, protocols)

- **NSF**: Joint research program of CISE and ENG directorates addressing CPS challenges in three areas (foundations; methods and tools; and components, run-time substrates, and systems); form partnerships to support advanced manufacturing through CPS research that helps better integrate IT into manufactured goods; core research in software and information foundations, communications, and computer systems; Expeditions projects in next-generation approaches to software and system assurance and CPS; Secure and Trustworthy Computing (SaTC) to ensure security, reliability, privacy, and usability; create core disciplinary, exploratory, and educational programs; and the National Robotics Initiative (NRI) to accelerate the development and use of robotics cooperatively with people

- **OSD**: Improve the DoD's ability to design, build, test, and sustain software-intensive cyber-physical systems that meet DoD mission-critical requirements for embedded and distributed systems, exhibit predictable behavior, and enable affordable evolution and interoperability; includes specification of complex requirements; "correct-by-construction" software development; scalable composition; high-confidence software and middleware; system architectures for network-centric environments; technologies for system visualization, testing, verification, and validation; model- and platform-based design and development approaches; and tools for controlling automated exploration and evaluation of massive trade spaces

High End Computing Infrastructure and Applications (HEC I&A)

NITRD Agencies: DoD (HPCMP), DoD Service Research Organizations, DOE/NNSA, DOE/SC, NASA, NIH, NIST, NOAA, NSF, and OSD

HEC I&A agencies coordinate Federal activities to provide advanced supercomputing systems, applications software, extreme-scale data management and analysis, and HEC R&D infrastructure to meet Federal agency mission needs and support national competitiveness. HEC infrastructure enables researchers in academia, industry, and Federal institutions to model and simulate complex processes in aerospace, astronomy, biology, biomedical science, chemistry, climate and weather, energy and environmental sciences, materials science, measurement science, nanoscale science and technology, national security, physics, and other areas to make breakthrough scientific and technological discoveries, address national priorities, and meet Federal agency mission needs. In addition to solving the most complex problems and enabling new insights and discoveries, advances in HEC technologies impact the entire spectrum of computing devices, from the largest systems to hand-held devices, allowing the most powerful computing platforms to become more affordable and smaller devices more powerful over time. The Federal HEC infrastructure also serves as a critical enabler of diverse initiatives associated with national priorities such as cybersecurity, big data, climate science, nanotechnology, understanding the human brain, the Materials Genome Initiative, and advanced manufacturing.

President's FY 2015 Request

Strategic Priorities Underlying this Request

Investments in Federal HEC facilities, advanced applications, and next-generation systems support national competitiveness and provide the means for industry, academia, and Federal laboratories to apply advanced computational capabilities in support of Federal agencies' diverse science, engineering, and national security missions. They also provide the government with the flexibility and expertise to meet new challenges as they emerge. Priorities include:

- **Leadership-class and production-quality HEC systems**: Provide HEC systems with capabilities needed to meet critical agency mission needs and support the national science and engineering research communities, U.S. industry, and academic research; ensure that emerging computer technologies support industrial, national security, and scientific applications and reduce energy requirements for and climate impact of computing technology at all scales. U.S. leadership in HEC systems is critical for maintaining US competitiveness as a growing number of nations around the world increase their investments to develop and deploy HEC systems and applications

- **Advancement of HEC applications**: Support the development of scientific and engineering algorithms and applications software and tools for current and next-generation HEC platforms; develop mission-responsive computational environments; and lead critical applied research in algorithms and software for emerging architectures that are incompatible with existing codes

- **Leading-edge cyberinfrastructure**: Provide efficient, effective, and dependable access to HEC facilities and resources for user communities across a wide variety of skills and backgrounds in industry, academia, and Federal institutions; develop capabilities and enhance infrastructure for computational and data-enabled science, modeling, simulation, and analysis; and share best practices for managing and enhancing HEC resources in a cost-effective and energy-efficient manner

- **Broadening impact**: Conduct crosscutting activities by the HEC I&A agencies, individually or collectively, that span multiple major priorities and serve to extend the breadth and impact of high end computing to meet the nation's highest science, engineering, national security, and competitiveness priorities

Highlights of the Request

The HEC I&A agencies report the following areas as highlights of their planned investments for FY 2015 under each of the main HEC I&A priorities. Agencies are listed in alphabetical order:

- **Leadership-class and production-quality HEC systems**

  - **DoD (HPCMP)**: Provide continuously refreshed, large-scale, stable computational resources in DoD supercomputing centers nationwide that meet both capacity and capability needs. Procurement of large-scale enterprise HPC systems for DoD research, development, test, and evaluation (RDT&E) community (multiple multi-PF systems). Provide application support, data analysis and visualization, and HPC system expertise at five DoD Supercomputing Resource Centers

  - **DOE/NNSA**: Executing next round of commodity technology systems procurement; accepting hardware delivery of LANL/SNL Trinity Advanced Technology System

  - **DOE/SC**: Continue to provide computational resources to DOE/SC and the Nation through high performance production and leadership-class computing systems. Planned facilities upgrades will be initiated with long lead-time activities for 75 PF - 200 PF upgrades at each Leadership Computing Facility; NERSC will begin acceptance testing of the NERSC-8 system at LBNL

  - **NASA**: Upgrade HEC resources to satisfy NASA's growing scientific research and engineering requirements; broaden HEC services to support massive and embarrassingly parallel data analytical workload

  - **NIH**: Continued support for broad-based HEC I&A for biomedical computing applications. Extension and modernization of NIH campus high end computing facilities and networking, predominantly to serve the intramural community

  - **NOAA**: Continue to operate Gaea – 1100 TF Climate Computing HPC at DOE/ORNL; Zeus – 383 TF Weather and Climate HPC; Jet – Hurricane Forecast Improvement Project (HFIP) (roughly equivalent to 340 TF); allocation on DOE/SC's Titan HPC (roughly equivalent to 500 TF). Planning for FY 2015 system installation from Hurricane Sandy supplemental funding

  - **NSF**: New 2 PF compute resource Comet operational at SDSC in January 2016; new 10 PB data resource Wrangler operational at TACC in January 2016; Stampede fully operational (11 PF) – all Intel Xeon Phi coprocessors up and running; Kraken, Keeneland, Trestles, Gordon, and Lonestar awards expire – some might be extended based on review results; NSF Leadership class system Blue Waters fully operational, >1 PF sustained and 11.5 PF peak; Stampede, OSG, Yellowstone continuing. New solicitation to be issued in 2014 with deployment of a resource in January of 2016

- **Advancement of HEC applications**

  - **DoD (HPCMP)**: Mature and demonstrate large-scale software development and system management applications. Multi-physics applications development for acquisition engineering community in air vehicles, ground vehicles, ships, and RF antennas; training and university technology transfer; programming environments, system software, and computational skills transfer for both DoD workforce development and S&T application modernization. Frontier Projects combining multi-billion hour allocations with tech transfer and development to advance state-of-the-practice in the application of HPC to the DoD's most challenging problems

  - **DOE/NNSA**: Explore code transition/re-write options for extreme-scale readiness via co-design; investigate embedded UQ methodologies for multicore architectures

  - **DOE/SC**: R&E prototype plans for extreme scale - Fund second phase of FastForward research (develop prototypes of the most promising mid-term technologies from the FastForward program for further testing; incorporate near-term technologies from FastForward into planned facility upgrades at NERSC, ALCF and OLCF); computational partnerships for co-design; applied mathematics research (data-intensive science, UQ at extreme-scale computations, resilient solvers) ; prepare early science applications for use with planned facility upgrades

- o **NASA:** Application enhancement, data analysis, data management, and visualization support for advanced modeling in aerospace, earth science, and astrophysics

- o **NIH:** Scientific computing efforts such as biomolecular modeling, physiological modeling, and multiscale modeling that use HEC resources or are in pre-HEC state; biodata management and analysis

- o **NIST:** Measurement science to speed development and industrial applications of advanced materials; Materials Genome Initiative (development of modeling and simulation techniques, tools; VVUQ); Advanced Materials Center of Excellence (modeling and informatics to accelerate materials discovery and deployment); measurement infrastructure for HEC software (VVUQ); measurement science for visualization (hardware - uncertainty quantification, calibration, and correction; software - uncertainty quantification and visual representation, quantitative methods in visualization)

- o **NOAA:** Improve model-based computing of weather forecasting, hurricane forecasting, and climate prediction; ensemble forecasts, ecosystem forecasting, and integration with physics-based modules, hybrid architectures

- o **NSF:** CIF21 – Meta-program to coordinate the full cyber-ecosystem across NSF, advancing science and engineering through foundational research for managing, analyzing, visualizing, and extracting knowledge from massive datasets; CDS&E - Computational and Data Sciences and Engineering meta-program across many NSF units; SI^2 – long-term investment focused on catalyzing new thinking, paradigms, and practices in developing and using software, creating a software ecosystem that encompasses all levels of software and spans from embedded sensors to HEC to major instruments and facilities

- **Leading-edge cyberinfrastructure**

- o **DoD (HPCMP):** Defense Research and Engineering Network at 100 Gbps; collaborative development of cybersecurity tools; frameworks for productivity of non-expert users to enable broader application of HEC-enabled solutions

- o **DOE/NNSA:** Develop common computing environment across NNSA labs

- o **DOE/SC:** Continue emphasis on unified approaches to software, languages, and tools support to reduce barriers to effective use of complex HEC resources by application developers and users; continue operation of 100 Gbps testbed

- o **NASA:** Collaborate with industry to evaluate future advanced HEC system architectures. Continue developing the NASA Earth Exchange (NEX) collaborative computing platform, providing the geosciences community a complete work environment to access Earth observations, advanced computing resources, and a portal for sharing ideas, results, and workflows

- o **NIH:** Continue investment in scientific computing, e.g., software development, neuroscience solicitations, grid computing; NCI Cancer Genomics Cloud Pilots

- o **NOAA:** Leverage existing nationwide high-bandwidth, low-latency network to promote shared use of high performance computing across agencies

- o **NSF:** CIF21 – Meta-program to coordinate the full cyber-ecosystem across NSF, advancing science and engineering through foundational research for managing, analyzing, visualizing, and extracting knowledge from massive datasets; XSEDE – eXtreme Science and Engineering Discovery Environment:

CDS&E – Computational and Data Sciences and Engineering meta-program across many NSF units; SI^2 – long-term investment focused on catalyzing new thinking, paradigms, and practices in developing and using software, creating a software ecosystem that encompasses all levels of software and spans from embedded sensors to HEC to major instruments and facilities

- **Broadening impact**

  - **DoD (HPCMP)**: Develop next-generation computational workforce within DoD via skills development, deployment of both computational and domain-specific expertise to DoD RDT&E complex, and investments in tools and expertise that match HPC environments to user workflow

  - **HEC Agencies**: Verification & Validation, Uncertainty Quantification (VVUQ); improved user training

  - **NSF**: Education, training, and outreach activities led by the XSEDE award supporting the current and next generation workforce

Planning and Coordination Supporting Request

Since 2005, the HEC agencies have provided tens of billions of computing hours on the Nation's most powerful computing platforms to enable researchers from academia and industry to address ultra-complex scientific challenges; coordinating this activity remains a major focus of collaboration among the HEC agencies and these stakeholders. Another key focus is selecting, evaluating, procuring, and operating Federal high-end platforms – a complicated, labor-intensive process that the HEC agencies work closely together to streamline. A third major focus of collaborative activities is development of sharable computational approaches for investigation and analysis across the sciences. Cooperative activities under each of the HEC I&A strategic priorities include:

- **Leadership-class HEC systems**

  - **Access to leadership-class computing**: Coordination to make highest capability HEC resources available to the broad research community and industry – DoD (HPCMP), DOE/NNSA, DOE/SC, NASA, NIST, NOAA, and NSF

  - **System reviews, benchmarking, metrics**: Collaborations – DoD (HPCMP), DOE/NNSA, DOE/SC, NASA, NOAA, NSA, and NSF

  - **DOE intra-agency collaborations**: Joint system procurements for next advanced technology systems delivered in 2015 and 2017 – DOE/NNSA and DOE/SC

- **Advancement of HEC applications**

  - **DOE intra-agency collaborations**: SciDAC 3 institutes and partnerships continue – DOE/NNSA and DOE/SC

  - **Multiscale modeling in biomedical, biological, and behavioral systems**: Interagency collaboration to advance modeling of complex living systems – DoD, NIH, and NSF

  - **INCITE**: Over 5 billion core hours provided for projects such as climate, weather, and water model runs – DOE/SC and NOAA, and study of flow of suspensions – DOE/SC and NIST

  - **XSEDE, Petascale Computing Resource Allocations (PRAC)**: Provide 4-5 billion compute hours to the open science community - All disciplines represented

  - **Computational toxicology**: Integration of HEC technologies with molecular biology to improve methods for risk assessment of chemicals – DoD, DOE/SC, FDA, and NIH

  - **Earth System Modeling Framework (ESMF)**: DoD, DOE/SC, NASA, NOAA, and NSF

  - **Simulation study of cement hydration**: NIST and NSF

- **Leading-edge cyberinfrastructure**
  - **Remote Sensing Information Gateway (RSIG)**: Allows users to integrate their selected environmental datasets into a unified visualization – DOE/SC, NASA, and NOAA

- **Broadening impact**
  - **Interagency participation in proposal review panels, principal investigator meetings** – HEC agencies
  - **DOE best practices workshop series:** Develop and share best practices for HEC operations – DOE/NNSA, DOE/SC, and HEC agencies
  - **Competitiveness**: Broaden use of HEC and advanced modeling and simulation by U.S. engineering and manufacturing industries to expand advanced manufacturing capabilities across small, medium, and large business sectors – HEC IWG
  - **Strategic planning**: Update the 2004 High End Computing Revitalization Task Force strategic plan for U.S. HEC – HEC IWG
  - **Education/workforce development**: Infuse 21st century curriculum in HEC and computational science into academia; define a framework for development of the existing workforce that addresses HEC skills for both next-generation providers and users of HEC based on Federal HEC agency requirements; develop a Federal HEC inventory/portal for educational resources – HEC IWG
  - **Metrics**: Explore alternatives to Linpack benchmark to establish more meaningful measures for performance of U.S. HEC systems – HEC IWG
  - **Green computing**: Promote energy-efficient "green" computing practices and explore methods to dramatically reduce HEC energy consumption and related energy costs – DoD (HPCMP), DOE/SC, and NASA
  - **Technology transfer:** Transfer of computational skills and technologies to partners in industry and academia – HEC agencies

Additional 2014 and 2015 Activities by Agency

The following list provides a summary of individual agencies' ongoing programmatic interests for 2014 and 2015 under the HEC I&A PCA:

- **DoD (HPCMP):** HEC services for RDT&E community (e.g., platforms, computational science software support); computational science institutes for DoD priorities (air armament, health force protection, weather prediction, ground sensors, space situational awareness, rotorcraft, networks, microwaves, and munitions)

- **DOE/NNSA**: Operate ASC Cielo system (1.3 PF) at LANL and Sequoia system (20 PF) at LLNL while executing next round of commodity technology systems procurement

- **DOE/SC**: ASCR SciDAC Committee of Visitors (COV) scheduled for FY 2014; NERSC/SC program offices requirements reviews; operate Hopper (1.3 PF) and Edison (2.4 PF) systems at LBNL, the Mira system (10 PF) at ANL, and the Titan (27 PF) system at ORNL; prepare for upgrades at each site

- **NASA**: Augment Pleiades supercomputer at NAS (NASA Ames) in early FY 2014 (to 3.5 PF peak); continue to pursue Xeon Phi acceleration of selected applications; explore private and public cloud-bursting capability in HEC environment

- **NIH**: Fund predominantly broad-based biocomputing awards; implement recommendations, as directed, based on the Final report to The Advisory Committee to the Director, NIH, by the Data and Informatics Working Group

- **NIST**: Parallel and distributed algorithms and tools for measurement science, including fundamental mathematics, uncertainty quantification, image analysis, materials science, and virtual measurement laboratory

- **NOAA**: Detailed design and planning for next-generation NOAA research HPC architecture

- **NSF:** Support throughout the agency of computational and data science and engineering via the CDS&E meta-program. Program supports HEC software projects co-funded by a number of Directorates

High End Computing Research and Development (HEC R&D)

NITRD Agencies: DARPA, DoD (HPCMP), DoD Service Research Organizations, DOE/NNSA, DOE/SC, EPA, NASA, NIH, NIST, NOAA, NSA, NSF, and OSD
Other Participants: IARPA

HEC R&D agencies conduct and coordinate hardware and software R&D to enable the successful development and effective use of future high-end systems to support national competitiveness and to meet projected Federal agency mission needs. HEC R&D takes aim at many of society's long-term challenges and contributes to strengthening the Nation's leadership in science, engineering, and technology across computational platforms at all scales. Research areas of interest include promising departures from today's computational systems such as quantum information science, superconducting computing, and biological computing; system software, applications, and system architectures that effectively utilize billion-way concurrency; reducing the energy per computation by orders of magnitude; achieving system resilience at extreme scales; and enabling future revolutions in simulation and big-data-enabled applications and technology.

President's FY 2015 Request

Strategic Priorities Underlying This Request

For decades, HEC R&D agencies have led development of increasingly capable computing technologies and environments that have impacted the entire computing industry. These advances not only enhanced mission success but also enabled and motivated increased HEC usage by industry and academia, promoting economic competitiveness, national security, and scientific leadership. Now, the HEC community faces great challenges in creating effective high-end systems using technology that is driven by the consumer marketplace. New high-end systems will require advances in energy efficiency, data movement, concurrency, resilience, and programmability. These challenges must be met to achieve and exploit the orders of magnitude increase in HEC capability that are needed to solve increasingly data-intensive and complex problems for science, engineering, manufacturing, and national security. To address the growing complexity and long-term costs of emerging platforms, HEC researchers seek to exploit heterogeneous advanced processor technologies, novel memory and storage technologies, and innovative approaches to software creation, and to innovate to overcome challenges of energy consumption, reliability, and scalability. Given these challenges, the HEC R&D agencies see the following as key research priorities for FY 2015:

- **Extreme-scale computation**: Integrate computer science and applied mathematical foundations to address the challenges of productive and efficient computation at the exascale level and beyond. Develop innovative systems that combine increased speed, efficient use of energy, economic viability, high productivity, and robustness to meet future agency needs for systems that manage and analyze ultra-large volumes of data and run multiscale, multidisciplinary science and engineering simulations and national security applications. Explore new concepts and approaches for solving technical challenges such as power use, thermal management, file system I/O bottlenecks, resiliency, highly parallel system architectures with support for billion-way concurrency, and programming language and software development environments that can increase the usability and utility of large-scale multiprocessor (including hybrid) systems. Develop, test, and evaluate prototype HEC systems and software to reduce industry and end-user risk and to increase technological competitiveness. Implement critical technology R&D partnerships for extreme-scale readiness

- **New directions in HEC hardware, software, computer science, and system architectures**: Develop novel scientific frameworks, power-efficient system architectures, programming environments, measurement science, and hardware and software prototypes to take computing power and communications "beyond Moore's Law" and to advance potential new breakthroughs in biological, quantum, and superconducting computing

- **Productivity**: Continue collaborative development of new metrics of system performance, including benchmarking, lessons learned for acquisition, and reducing total ownership costs of HEC systems; integrate resources for improved productivity among all users. Design and develop requirements for software to enable, support, and increase the productivity of geographically dispersed collaborative teams that develop future HEC applications

- **Broadening impact**: Conduct crosscutting activities by the HEC R&D agencies, individually or collectively, that span multiple major priorities and serve to extend the breadth and impact of high end computing to meet the Nation's highest science, engineering, national security, and competitiveness priorities, including expanding the HPC workforce

Highlights of the Request

The HEC R&D agencies report the following areas as highlights of their planned research investments for FY 2015 under each of the main HEC R&D priorities. Agencies are listed in alphabetical order:

- **Extreme-scale computation**

  - **DARPA**: In 1965 Gordon E. Moore observed that, historically, the number of transistors on integrated circuits doubled approximately every two years. That trend, since named Moore's Law, endured for nearly five decades, but is now showing signs of age. DARPA investments aim to maintain the rate of advance in processing post-Moore's Law through new architectures, new packaging technologies, new interconnect technologies, new switching technologies, and better human interfaces

  - **DoD (HPCMP)**: Collaborative funding of application development environments and algorithms, runtime environments, and system software for extreme-scale computing

  - **DOE/NNSA**: Initiating next round of R&D vendor partnerships on co-design in order to analyze performance impacts by advanced architectures via proxy apps

  - **DOE/SC**: SciDAC institutes and partnerships, co-design for extreme-scale systems continues; computer science research for extreme-scale operating and runtime systems, software development environments, and software for data management, analysis, and visualization; research and evaluation prototypes for industry partnerships

  - **NSF**: Blue Waters project continues to support researchers requiring a sustained performance of > 1 PF on a broad set of applications

- **New directions in HEC hardware, software, computer science, and system architectures**

  - **DARPA**: Power efficient processing for embedded computing; photonic and next-generation electronic interconnects; 3D stacking; highly concurrent architectures; low power circuits and distributed switching voltage regulation; approximate computing; and proxy computing

  - **DoD (HPCMP)**: Augment stable, large-scale HPC systems with targeted special-purpose or emerging computational platforms for niche and future application-space requirements. Develop scalable, complex, multi-physics based codes for critical defense applications. Develop advanced cybersecurity tools and instrumentation

  - **DOE/NNSA**: Investments in identified R&D critical technologies to address extreme-scale barriers via R&D collaboration with DOE/SC

  - **DOE/SC**: Computer science research for: data-intensive science (develop new paradigm for generating and executing dynamic workflows that include the development of new workflow engines and languages that are semantically rich and allow interoperability or interchangeably in many environments; development of scalable and interactive visualization methods for ensembles, multivariate and multiscale data; define components and associated application programing interfaces for storing, annotating, and accessing scientific data; support development of standards); extreme-scale computing (X-Stack 3 on programming models and environments); storage systems and I/O

- **EPA**: Analytics and computer science required for extreme-scale, mission-related research programs in air quality, emissions, climate research, and interactions with human health; advanced, distributed, massive-volume data and modeling capabilities with initial applications to support world-class science; infrastructure to combine existing and future data at various and extreme temporal and spatial scales, run global models, and provide inputs and technology across computational platforms at all scales

- **IARPA**: Superconducting supercomputing

- **NASA**: Research and explore alternative HEC strategies such as emerging quantum computing systems, including quantum algorithms for hard, discrete optimization problems and their mapping to and embedding on quantum architectures

- **NIST**: Quantum information science and engineering; quantum information theory (quantum algorithms, complexity: assessing the true power of quantum resources); quantum computing assessment (techniques and tools to assess the capabilities of candidate technologies); quantum technology demonstrations (evaluating feasibility of applications of quantum resources in computing, communications)

- **NOAA**: Big data management, movement, error detection and correction, and analytics

- **NSA**: Advanced Computing Systems (ACS) research program; superconducting supercomputing; quantum computing

- **NSF**: Examine operating/runtime systems, development environments, productivity tools, languages, compilers, libraries (XPS); biological computing; cloud computing initiative

- **Productivity**

  - **DoD, DOE/SC, and NSF**: Capabilities for scientific research - computational concepts, methods, and tools for discovery. Centers, institutes, and partnerships for predictive and data-intensive science, applied math and computer science challenges of data-intensive science and scientific computing at extreme scale

  - **DOE/SC and NOAA**: Meta scheduling (Moab)

  - **NOAA**: Job queuing management (Grid)

- **Broadening impact**

  - **DoD (HPCMP)**: Partner with other Federal agencies in discovery and demonstration of algorithms, tools, libraries—as well as system management, workflow, and runtime systems—that will enable DoD productivity on next-generation extreme-scale hardware

Planning and Coordination Supporting Request

Coordination among the HEC R&D agencies focuses on computer science advancements to improve the performance and efficiency of the current generation of HEC hardware and software as well as on avenues of fundamental research to create revolutionary new architectures and systems. The complexity of high-end hardware architectures, systems software, and supporting technologies is such that Federal program managers and researchers depend on the constant flow of information among colleagues and technical experts to keep current with developments, gain new knowledge, and share best practices and lessons learned. In addition to joint technical/planning workshops and proposal/technical reviews that HEC R&D agencies routinely conduct, the following are selected examples of the scope of interagency collaboration under each of the HEC R&D strategic priorities:

- **Extreme-scale computation**
  - **Joint workshops on extreme-scale resilience**: DoD, DOE/NNSA, and DOE/SC
  - **DOE intra-agency collaborations**: Critical R&D investments in memory, processors, storage, interconnects, systems engineering, etc.; joint development work to fully address the parallelism, power, memory, and data movement issues associated with multicore computing at the exascale level – DOE/NNSA and DOE/SC
  - **Computing MOU:** DoD, DOE/NNSA, and DOE/SC
  - **Extreme-scale R&D technologies and Modeling/Simulation Working Group:** HEC agencies
  - **Big data:** Explore synergies and convergences between HEC and the Big Data realm to ensure HEC capabilities support the many emerging data-intensive applications and domains – HEC agencies

- **New directions in HEC hardware, software, computer science, and system architectures**
  - **Quantum information theory and science**: Study information, communication, and computation based on devices governed by the principles of quantum physics – DARPA, IARPA, NASA, NIST, NSA, and NSF
  - **Superconducting (cryogenic) supercomputing:** IARPA and NSA
  - **Cloud-based HPC:** Explore supercomputing in the cloud through public and private service providers to determine applicability/efficiencies for subset of Federal HEC needs – NASA and NSF
  - **Extreme-scale system software R&D co-funding:** DoD (HPCMP), DOE/NNSA, and DOE/SC
  - **3D stacked memory project**: DOE/NNSA and DOE/SC
  - **Source code porting and scaling studies:** Collaborations for weather and climate models – NASA, NOAA, and TACC

- **Productivity**
  - **Benchmarking and performance modeling**: Collaborate on developing performance measurement test cases with applications commonly used by the Federal HEC community for use in system procurements, evaluation of Federal HEC system productivity – DoD (HPCMP), DOE/NNSA, DOE/SC, NASA, NSA, and NSF
  - **HEC metrics**: Coordinate on effective metrics for application development and execution on high-end systems – DoD, DOE/NNSA, DOE/SC, NASA, NSA, and NSF
  - **Meta scheduling:** Moab – DOE/SC and NOAA
  - **Job queuing management:** Grid – NOAA

- **Broadening impact**
  - **HEC hardware and software:** Facilitate access to and share knowledge gained and lessons learned from HEC hardware and software development efforts – DoD, DOE/NNSA, DOE/SC, EPA, NASA, NIST, NOAA, and NSF
  - **HEC tools:** Coordinate R&D in operating/runtime systems, development environments, productivity tools, languages, compilers, libraries – DARPA, DOE/NNSA, DOE/SC, NASA, NSA, and NSF
  - **HEC data challenges:** Coordinate with NITRD HCI&IM CG, LSN CG, and Big Data SSG and IWG on Digital Data – HEC agencies
  - **Workforce development planning**: HEC IWG and NITRD SEW-Ed agencies
  - **ASCR Committee of Visitors review of computer science program:** DOE/SC and NSF

Additional 2014 and 2015 Activities by Agency

The following list provides a summary of individual agencies' ongoing programmatic interests for 2014 and 2015 under the HEC R&D PCA:

- **DARPA:** Develop the technologies and techniques to overcome the power efficiency barriers that currently constrain embedded computing system capabilities; create new architectures, new packaging technologies, new interconnect technologies, new switching technologies, and better human interfaces

- **DoD (HPCMP):** HEC systems and software R&D in support of DoD mission priorities; modeling and simulation; user productivity; investigations into fundamentally new ways of expressing parallelism to address the strong scaling problem for current and future large scale hardware

- **DOE/SC:** Extreme Scale research PI meeting scheduled for FY 2014

- **NASA:** Prototype energy efficient green computing systems using warm water to cool computing components; SBIR subtopic seeking advanced HEC technologies for enhanced productivity; efficient computing – sustained performance per dollar or watt; integrated environments for enhanced user productivity; ultrascale computing – overcoming the challenges of massive concurrency, software/system co-design, and application V&V

- **NIST:** Quantum information theory (algorithms for simulation of quantum field theories; analysis of quantum cryptographic devices); quantum computing assessment (randomized benchmarks for testing fidelity of multi-qubit gates; quantum state tomography); quantum technology demonstrations (develop/assess quantum memory/communications interface technologies; develop specialized quantum devices, e.g., random number generators whose values are certified to be unknown before measurement)

- **NOAA:** Continue collaborative involvement with Earth Systems Modeling Framework (ESMF); improve techniques for transitioning codes from research to operations; improve speed, accuracy, integrity of data transfer for large data sets; explore optimal configurations for grid and meta scheduler

- **NSA:** ACS research program changed from thrust-centric to end-to-end centric for modeling, simulation, emulation; computer architecture and engineering; mission proxies; system level metrics (energy, productivity, resilience); SME collaborations (machine learning, file I/O, runtime systems, memory, and storage, etc.); superconducting supercomputing; quantum computing

- **NSF:** CIF21, software and data-enabled science and education (NSF Research Traineeship); cyber-physical systems; advanced manufacturing; cybersecurity - SaTC; computing workforce; high performance computing and storage services; technical audit service - gather data and evaluate HPC; XSEDE integrating services (coordination and management service, extended collaborative support service, training, education, and outreach service); Open Science Grid (cyberinfrastructure, virtual organization)

Human Computer Interaction and Information Management (HCI&IM)

NITRD Agencies: AHRQ, DARPA, DoD Service Research Organizations, EPA, NARA, NASA, NIH, NIST, NOAA, NSF, and OSD
Other Participants: USDA, USGS, and VA

HCI&IM focuses on R&D to expand human capabilities to use and manage data and information through the use of computer hardware, software, and systems technologies. These technologies include robotics, visualization agents, cognitive systems, collaborative systems, and others that support the organization and the journey from data to knowledge to action. Scientific research, energy and the environment, climate change and prediction, healthcare, education and training, protecting our information infrastructure, emergency planning and response, national defense, homeland security, weather forecasting, and space exploration are just some of the national priorities that HCI&IM research helps facilitate and improve.

HCI&IM research spans both the technologies that enable people to access and use digital information (HCI) and those that expand the capabilities of computing systems and devices to acquire, store, process, and make accessible data and information for humans to use (IM). Transformative approaches for accessing, extracting meaning from and displaying data remains a critical need because the volume, variety, and velocity of data are quickly overtaking the technical capabilities to process, manage, and analyze it. The Federal Government generates and maintains the world's largest digital collections of science and engineering data, historical records, health information, and scientific and other types of archival literature. Rapid knowledge discovery requires next-generation methods, technologies, and tools that integrate and efficiently manage massive stores of streaming, distributed, heterogeneous information while integrating the human in the discovery process. Such capabilities are essential for U.S. economic growth and technological innovation.

President's FY 2015 Request

Strategic Priorities Underlying This Request

Strategic priorities in HCI&IM include:

- **Data Visualization:** Requirements for the enhancement of visualization tools used in collaborative and multi-user environments to better enable decision making and understanding of large data sets through increased usability

- **Human engagement and decision making systems:**

  - **New methods** to make large, diverse, and streaming data sets meaningful to analysts and decision makers in a timely way

  - **Personalization** that requires human-performance modeling, multimodal interfaces, and mechanisms for distributed collaboration, knowledge management, virtual organizations, and visual environments. There is a crosslink to cognitive and perceptual process modeling and measurement

- **Information integration:**

  - **Decision support systems** provide mechanisms for sifting through large, complex data sets to identify alternative strategies from the data that, without computational analysis, would strain human cognitive capabilities

  - **Information management systems** enable individuals and organizations to create, share, and apply information to gain value and achieve specific objectives and priorities

- **Standards** provide a way for data to be brought together with shared meaning, providing the basis for interoperability and relationship building which is a basic step of integrating and managing data

- **Information infrastructure**: A robust, resilient national digital data framework for long-term preservation and accessibility of electronic records as well as expanding data and records collections

Highlights of the Request

The HCI&IM agencies report the following areas as highlights of their planned R&D investments for FY 2015. Agencies are listed in alphabetical order:

- **From big data to new knowledge and action**: Analysis R&D requires not only new computing research in models, algorithms, and tools to accelerate scientific discovery and productivity from heterogeneous, ultra-scale data stores, but also development of innovative, multidimensional approaches to highly complex data. For complex data, new ways should be developed to enable the intuitive display of complex interactions and mechanisms that enhance both discovery and use of data, as well as effective analytical products for decision makers and the public – AHRQ, DARPA, DoD Service research organizations, EPA, NARA, NASA, NIH, NIST, NOAA, NSF, OSD, and other agencies

- **Human engagement and decision**: Design effective HCI and systems integration that provide personalization. This requires human-performance modeling, multimodal interfaces, and mechanisms for distributed collaboration, knowledge management, virtual organizations, and visual environments. There is a crosslink to cognitive and perceptual process modeling and measurement. Expand virtual reality technologies for simulation and training as well as biometric and voting systems – DoD Service research organizations, EPA, NASA, NIST, NOAA, NSF, and OSD

- **Effective stewardship of science and engineering data**: This effort will maximize the value gained from current and previous Federal investments but will require additional research in providing for life-cycle stewardship over time. Research foci include personalized access to information, as well as federation, preservation, curation, data life-cycle stewardship, and analysis of large, heterogeneous collections of scientific data, information, and records. A persistent issue is the need for fault-tolerant, scalable management of information input and output in light of new system architectures – EPA, NARA, NASA, NIH, NIST, NOAA, NSF, and other agencies

- **Information integration, accessibility, and management**: Multiple advances are required in technologies, system architectures, and tools for optimized, scalable ingest and processing for high-capacity data integration (especially of Geographic Information System (GIS) and spatio-temporal data), management, exploitation, modeling, and analysis. In addition, investigation continues in cloud-based infrastructures to efficiently gain distributed access to data resources utilizing new ontologies and metadata formats for discovery – AHRQ, DARPA, EPA, NARA, NASA, NIH, NIST, NOAA, and NSF

- **Earth/space science data and information systems**: These efforts enable multiagency access to and use of Federal scientific data resources through Web-based tools and services (e.g., remote visualization) that exploit advances in computer science and technology – EPA, NASA, NOAA, NSF, and other agencies

- **Health information technologies**: NITRD's Health IT R&D SSG is developing guidance for R&D in this area. Research needs that have been identified include expansion of clinical decision-support systems, development of more effective use of electronic health records and data, and defining national health information and device interoperability standards – AHRQ, FDA, CMS, NIH, NIST, NSF, ONC, and other agencies

- **Information search and retrieval**: New research methods and tools are necessary for evaluation and performance measures of information-discovery technologies, as well as relevance feedback. Current focus areas include legal discovery, recognition of opinion, and patent search, as well as domain-specific search and machine reading of records – DARPA, NARA, NIST, and NSF

- **Cognitive, adaptive, and intelligent systems**: Algorithmic and multidisciplinary research is designed to discover the cognitive, perceptual modeling for joint cognitive systems design; autonomy, trustworthiness, and reliability of automated systems; engineered intelligence and adaptability; robotics, human-robot teaming; automated computational intelligence; affective computing – DARPA, DoD Service research organizations, NARA, NASA, NIST, NSF, and OSD

- **Multimodal language recognition and translation**: Improve multilingual language technology performance in areas of speech-to-text transcription and text-to-text transcription. A goal is to provide spontaneous two-way communications translation, machine reading, text retrieval, document summarization/distillation, automatic content extraction, and speaker and language recognition through multimodal interfaces – DARPA, DoD Service research organizations, NARA, NASA, NIST, NSF, and OSD

Planning and Coordination Supporting Request

Although the HCI&IM portfolio includes a broad range of enabling technologies, the current focus of coordination among the agencies is the overriding challenge of ultra-scale, heterogeneous data: how to manage it, enable interoperability and usability, and develop new infrastructures and tools that broaden access and exploration to a wider range of end users. The following HCI&IM collaborations seek to forward this agenda:

- **Foundations of visualization and analysis**: This provides a multiagency mechanism for coordination of research in feature extraction for anomaly detection, integration of multiple types of data and records at scale or format, the use of visualization as an interface, and biomedical imaging. The upcoming "Frontiers of Visualization" meeting series, focusing on topics of adequacy of visualization for decision support, cognitive bias in decision making, and cross-cultural influences on visualization, is expected to produce top research questions in various knowledge areas – AHRQ, EPA, NARA, NASA, NIH, NIST, NOAA, NSF, and other agencies

- **Science and Science Innovation Policy Interagency Task Group**: Coordination on Federal science policy issues and metrics – HCI&IM agencies and others

- **Biodiversity and Ecosystem Informatics Task Group**: The group provides an ongoing Federal point of contact and body for cooperation, with a focus on aspects of environmental, natural resources, and sustainability as outlined in the President's Council of Advisors on Science and Technology (PCAST) July 2011 report *Sustaining Environmental Capital: Protecting Society and the Economy* – DoD, DOE/SC, EPA, Interior, NASA, NIH, NOAA, NSF, and other agencies

- **Earth/space science, climate, and weather**: Agencies focus on cooperative activities in providing interoperable data (including through the Big Earth Data Initiative), multidimensional models, and tools for better understanding and prediction based on the growing corpus of observational and experimental data – DoD Service research organizations, EPA, NASA, NOAA, NSF, OSD, and other agencies

- **National Robotics Initiative**: Innovative robotics research and applications that emphasize the realization of co-robots acting in direct support of, or in a symbiotic relationship with, human partners – NASA, NIH, NSF, and USDA

- **Information access, management, and preservation**: Multiple agencies participate in the IWG on Digital Data and the IWG on Public Access to Scientific Publications. Topics of consideration include new policy development and identification of existing standards for interoperability, such as the Digital Preservation Interoperability Framework International Standard (DPIF). Agencies have also been called to meet requirements identified in the Presidential Records Management Directive focusing on electronic recordkeeping – EPA, NARA, NASA, NIH, NIST, NOAA, NSF, and other agencies

- **Usability**: People are the ultimate users of information. Usability research draws input from the social and behavioral sciences and informs the design and evaluation of technical solutions with the goal of ease of use. Research areas include health IT, security, voting, biometrics systems, and decision-support systems – AHRQ, NIST, and NSF

Additional 2014 and 2015 Activities by Agency

The following list provides a summary of individual agencies' ongoing programmatic interests for 2014 and 2015 under the HCI&IM PCA:

- **AHRQ**: Quality measurement and improvement; healthcare decision making; patient and clinician information needs; and U.S. Health Information Knowledgebase ; Evidence-based practice center reports

- **DARPA**: Automatically translate large volumes of foreign-language speech and text, including informal genres (e.g., online discussion groups, messaging, and telephone conversation); automatically collate, filter, synthesize, summarize, and present relevant information in near real-time; new domain-specific search paradigms to discover content relevant to specific missions and tasks; create computer programming technologies that greatly facilitate the construction of new machine learning applications in a wide range of domains; create new approaches to automated computational intelligence that create abstract yet predictive—ideally causal—models from massive volumes of diverse data

- **EPA**: Databases for computational toxicology; scientific information management (tools, best practices for management, accessibility of complex EPA data sets); distributed environmental applications; and air quality forecasting

- **NARA**: Global-scale capable, open source, "next generation" cloud technologies, architectures, and services enabling effective sustainable management, intellectual control, and access to nationally distributed billion file and larger scale complex digital object collections

- **NASA**: Earth Science Data collaborative systems; basic and applied research in human performance; decision-support technologies for NextGen; multimodal interface research; research on advanced tools for discovering tools and services, and developing as well as preserving provenance of data products and associated information

- **NIH**: Collaborative Research in Computational Neuroscience (CRCNS) Innovative Approaches to Science and Engineering Research on Brain Function; Big Data Centers of Excellence; Analysis of Genome-Wide Fene-Environment (GxE) Interactions; focus areas include decision making for patients and clinicians, natural language understanding, organization and retrieval of health-related information by consumers, visualization and mapping of heterogeneous data for clinical researchers, support for healthy behaviors, and device interfaces

- **NIST**: Biometrics evaluation, usability, and standards (fingerprint, face, iris, voice/speaker); multimedia evaluation methods (video retrieval, audio and video analysis); measurement, evaluation tools for 3D shape searching; data preservation metrology, standards; usability of voting and security systems; manufacturing, supply chain informatics; standards for manufacturing robots; engineering informatics sustainability; computational biology; mathematical knowledge management

- **NOAA**: Technologies for real-time weather/climate data in multiple formats for scientists, forecasters, first responders, and citizens; remote visualization via N-Wave, new high-definition devices; disaster planning, mitigation, response, and recovery

- **NSF**: Through academic R&D, NSF supports CIF21 as well as programs in support of information privacy, data and open publication access, ubiquitous networked data environments, human-computer partnerships, socially intelligent computing, understanding the science of information, cognition mechanisms in human learning, and remote access to experimental facilities

Large Scale Networking (LSN)

NITRD Agencies: AFRL, AHRQ, DARPA, DHS, DoD (CERDEC, DREN, HPCMP), DOE/SC, NASA, NIH, NIST, NOAA, NSA, NSF, ONR, and OSD

LSN members coordinate Federal agency networking R&D in leading-edge networking technologies, services, and enhanced performance, including programs in fundamental networking research, future Internet architectures, heterogeneous multimedia testbeds and demonstrations; end-to-end performance and performance measurement; network security; software defined networks, wireless networks, and networks for disaster response; the science and engineering of complex networks; networking tools and services for cloud, grid, and collaboration; advanced networking components; networking education, training, and outreach; and the engineering and management of large-scale networks for scientific and applications R&D, including capabilities for large-scale data transfer and virtual organization functionality. The results of this coordinated R&D, once deployed, assure that the next-generation Internet will be scalable, reliable, and flexible.

President's FY 2015 Request

Strategic Priorities Underlying This Request

The missions of the LSN agencies, though varied, all require ultra-high-speed communications, ultra-scale data-transfer capabilities, and collaboration capabilities with demanding constraints of end-to-end performance, security, reliability, resilience, and availability. The advanced Federal research networks support national security needs as well as transport data among the world's leading science discipline centers and observational systems on the ground, on the seas, in the air, and in space. Each year, the LSN agencies identify a small number of priority areas in which focused research collaboration will promote advances in networking that address these needs and benefit all. The big data testbed, for example, identifies architectures and deploys best practices for transport of big data in support of advanced science applications. LSN collaborative activities for 2015 will focus on:

- **Enabling end-to-end big data applications:** Build on the big data testbed demonstrations of FY 2014 and expand the networking support of big data transfers, implement network performance technology, monitor the network performance and work with applications users to improve end-to-end throughput, reliability, and security of big data transfers

- **Operational capabilities:** Identify approaches, best practices, and testbed implementations for Software Defined Networking (SDN)/OpenFlow, tactical communications and network technologies (e.g., dynamic ad-hoc, multi-hop secure, robust wireless networks and data-centric environments), identity management, cloud computing, collaboration capabilities, spectrum management, IPv6, DNSSEC, science DMZ, and Trusted Internet Connections (TICs). Promote cooperation among network R&D testbeds and applications development including GENI, ANI, US Ignite, and others

- **Optical networking**: Coordinate the development and deployment of dynamic optical networking to support leading-edge science applications (e.g., technology, architecture, and infrastructure), multiple 100 Gbps connectivity for large data flows, and trans-Atlantic 100 Gbps lambdas

Highlights of the Request

The LSN agencies report the following topical areas as highlights of their planned networking R&D investments for FY 2015. Agencies are listed in alphabetical order:

- **Network architectures and protocols for future networks (FIA-NP, GENI, NeTS, CIF21):** Develop and test network architecture concepts to enable reliable, secure, flexible, dynamic, heterogeneous networking and hybrid networking capabilities, peer-to-peer capabilities, and support sustainable environments, energy-efficient networking, virtualization at scale, and mobile hotspots – AFRL, CERDEC, DARPA, DoD (HPCMP), DOE/SC, NASA, NIST, NSF, ONR, and OSD

- **Big data networking**: Develop and test terabit-plus end-to-end architecture and protocols for big data (integrated with storage, applications, and computational resources), e.g., science DMZ, SATCOM – DOE/SC, NASA, NOAA, NSA, and NSF

- **SDN and OpenFlow technology:** Develop, deploy, and operate security, interdomain, layers 1, 2, and 3 operational capability – DOE/SC, NIST, NSA, and NSF

- **Wireless networking**: Develop standards and tools enabling better interconnectivity, seamless multidomain, heterogeneous, and layer interoperability; electronic warfare/communications coexistence and management for wideband (e.g., SWAP reduction, data fusion, heterogeneous interfaces, spectrum management and efficiency, sensing and sharing, mobile hotspots, constraints and efficiency, low probability of detection, and anti-jam); robust, secure, resilient, dynamic, mobile, DTN, spread-spectrum, LTE, WiMAX, airborne, and sensor networks – AFRL, CERDEC, DARPA, NASA, NIST, NSA, NSF, and ONR

- **Experimental network facilities**: Provide testbeds at differing scales, promote cooperation, and test advanced applications on DOE/SC's 100/400 Gigabit (Gb) ANI, NSF's GENI, international ANA 100G, and other R&D testbeds, to demonstrate performance at scale of new architectures (e.g., SDN and OpenFlow), end-to-end applications (e.g., US Ignite) and protocols – DOE/SC, NASA, NIST, NOAA, NSA, and NSF

- **Strategic technologies for networking**: Provide basic research, development, and demonstration of new technologies for robust, secure, reliable, evolvable, wired and wireless networking, underwater communications, autonomous dynamic ad hoc routing infrastructure, tactical networking, medical devices, and assistive technologies – CERDEC, DARPA, DOE/SC, NIST, NSA, NSF, and ONR

- **Cloud and grid computing**: Secure federated software tools and cloud services for multidomain collaboration, cyber-physical systems, data distribution and management, visualization, software stack for large-scale scientific collaborations, high-bandwidth implementation, interoperable smart grid standards and testbeds, Open Science Grid – DOE/SC, NASA, NIH, NIST, NOAA, NSA, and NSF

- **Computational research infrastructure (CC*IIE, IRNC, ESnet, N-Wave, Science DMZ, Hawaii and Alaska connectivity, NIH cancer and medical imaging support):** Provide networking to support U.S. and international research communities for networking research, large-scale data flows, health science, clinical support, and applications across all science disciplines – AHRQ, DoD (HPCMP), DOE/SC, NASA, NIH, NIST, NOAA, and NSF

- **Energy aware and efficient networks:** Develop energy efficient technology and architectures for end-to-end big data applications, ad hoc mobile wireless and sensor networking, and modeling for economic sustainability – AFRL, CERDEC, DOE/SC, NSA, NSF, and ONR

- **End-to-end network management:** Enable cross-domain end-to-end performance measurement for advanced networking; autonomous secure management; provide tools for and implement performance Services-Oriented Network Architecture (perfSONAR) – CERDEC, DOE/SC, NASA, NIST, and NSF

- **Network security research**: Develop technologies for detection of anomalous behavior; standards, modeling, and measurement to achieve end-to-end security over wireless networks, heterogeneous, multidomain networks and infrastructure; critical-infrastructure protection; trustworthy networking; privacy, confidentiality, authentication, policy; delay tolerant networking; and cryptography – AFRL, CERDEC, DARPA, DOE/SC, NASA, NIH, NIST, NSA, NSF, and ONR

- **Security implementation (Protected SATCOM, cybersecurity defenses, IPv6, DNSSEC, Delay-Tolerant Networking [DTN], Trusted Internet Connections [TICs]):** Develop and implement near-term mandated capabilities – DARPA, DOE/SC, DREN, NASA, NIH, NIST, NSA, and NSF

- **Complexity in networking:** Develop concepts, methods, architectures, protocols, and measurement for modeling networks as complex, autonomous, and dynamic systems – DARPA, DOE/SC, NIST, and NSF

- **Public-safety networking, disaster recovery, and crisis management**: Provide Disaster Information Management Research Center (DIMRC), public-safety communications, implant communication system – NIH (NLM) and NIST

Planning and Coordination Supporting Request

The LSN agencies have extensive experience working through interagency and private-sector partnerships to interconnect and extend the capabilities of Federally supported research networks. For example, by engaging participants from academia, industry, national labs, and international networking groups, LSN's Joint Engineering Team is able to coordinate efforts to resolve technical networking issues at the global level and to develop collaborative testbeds for exploring advanced technologies at scale. In summary, the following are ongoing LSN coordination activities:

- **Interagency research agenda**: Networking and demonstrations for extreme-scale science and data flows; experimentation, network management, perfSONAR deployment; DTN; experimental design for complex systems; network performance measurement; network security; and GENI, OpenFlow, US Ignite, and SDN testing – LSN agencies

- **Infrastructure cooperation**: National and international connectivity and performance measurement – DOE/SC, DREN, NASA, NOAA, and NSF

- **Multiagency workshops**: Software Defined Networking; Scaling Terabit Networks, Future Directions in Wireless Networking Collaboration, Leveraging perfSONAR – Multiple agencies

- **400 Gbps/terabit networking research** – Multiple agencies

- **Transoceanic networking for science** – DOE/SC and NSF

- **Inter-service collaboration**: Research on robust, reliable, secure wireless and heterogeneous networking; spectrum access and management; DTN; and services for federation, management, information, discovery, and secure delivery mobile hotspots; Tactical Infrastructure Enterprise Services (TIES), Dynamic Tactical Communications Networks (DTCN) – AFRL, CERDEC, and ONR

- **Software defined networking:** Testing of SDN and OpenFlow applications in at-scale testbeds – DOE/SC, DREN, NIST, NSA, and NSF

- **Public safety communication research** – ITS, NIST, and NTIA

- **Coordination by LSN Teams**

  - **Joint Engineering Team (JET)**: Advanced testbeds, coordination of end-user requirements, science user interfaces, engineering of research networks and testbeds (JETnets); end-to-end big data transport and storage networks; security best practices, applications testbeds (DNSSEC, IPv6, performance measurement), TICs coordination; interdomain and end-to-end metrics, monitoring; tool sharing and exchange; international coordination; and transit and services cooperation – DOE/SC, DREN, NASA, NIH, NIST, NOAA, NSA, NSF, and ONR

  - **Middleware And Grid Interagency Coordination (MAGIC) Team**: Cloud computing services, grid computing services, middleware; cloud and grid standards and implementation status (TeraGrid, Open Science Grid [OSG], Earth Systems Grid [ESG]); best practices for resource architecture, access, and management; security and privacy, e.g., identity management; and international coordination – DOE/SC, NASA, NIST, and NSF

- **Information exchange**: Multiagency participation in review panels, informational meetings, principal investigator (PI) meetings; coordination among program managers; and joint JET, DOE Energy Sciences Network Steering Committee (ESSC) and Internet2 Joint Techs Meetings – AFOSR, DARPA, DOE/SC, NASA, NIST, NSA, NSF, and ONR

- **Partnerships for research connectivity** – DOE/SC, DREN, NASA, NOAA, and NSF

Additional 2014 and 2015 Activities by Agency

The following list provides a summary of individual agencies' ongoing programmatic interests for 2014 and 2015 under the LSN PCA:

- **AFRL**: Tactical airborne links and networks, global, interference tolerant, tactical embedded information management, spectrum efficient agile networks, wideband airborne communications, cross-domain information sharing, tactical wireless, secure cross-domain information sharing and collaboration, information brokering for embedded platforms, mission responsive information services

- **AHRQ**: Personal Health Information Management (PHIM) tools; with CMS, ONC, NIH (NLM) - United States Health Information Knowledgebase (USHIK)

- **CERDEC**: Protected SATCOM, size, weight, and power (SWAP) reduction, communications/electronic warfare co-existence, SDN, DTN, dynamic spread spectrum, communications in a contested electronic warfare environment, SATCOM extension to tactical maneuver platforms, increased bandwidth, interference resistance, dynamic spread spectrum, inter-domain routing

- **DARPA**: Wireless Network after Next (WNaN) and Advanced Wireless Networks for the Soldier (AWNS) programs

- **DREN**: Implement network services (IPv6, DNSSEC, TICs, NTP, VTC; develop/deploy cyber security defenses; SDN demos; advanced networking (DREN III); and network high-speed access to Alaska and Hawaii

- **DOE/SC**: SDN/OpenFlow for science applications, extreme-scale scientific knowledge discovery and software sustainability research, understanding applications on complex networks, multiple 100 Gbps end-to-end testing with science applications, 400 Gbps-Terabit networking, big data networking demonstrations, open exchange points (layers 1, 2, and 3), trans-Atlantic 100 Gbps lambdas

- **NASA**: Network access control, end-to-end QOS, TIC security monitoring, IT security, emerging technology, enterprise architecture, management governance, IPv6 transition, web proxies, and intrusion protection

- **NIH**: Advanced networking for health science research, clinical needs and disaster management, networking for biomedical computing (Big Data to Knowledge [BD2K]), cancer imaging archive, network for medical image sharing, support for multi-parameter intelligent monitoring in intensive care database

- **NIST**: New network technology and architectures, develop measurement science and apply to network systems, public safety communications, Smart Grid communications, dynamic spectrum access, cloud computing and complex information systems, internet infrastructure protection, high assurance domains, measurement science for complex systems, wireless communications in alternative frequencies (GHz-THz), robust internet architectures, metrology for performance of network anomaly detection algorithms

- **NOAA**: N-Wave integration of and access to HPC and data centers, X-Wave external peering network, TICs, measurement and performance tools, preparation for 100 Gbps networking, expanded connectivity to small and medium sites, connectivity to next-generation satellite programs (JPSS, GOES-R), next generation of Next Generation Internet Exchange (NGIX) concept, shared network infrastructure including access to Alaska and Hawaii

- **NSA**: SDN (security focus), cloud computing, low SWAP Tbps networking, cyberdefense at scale, extreme data transport, critical infrastructures, delay-tolerant networking

- **NSF**: Innovative networking architectures to support application domains (NeTS, enterprise, core, optical wireless, cellular peer-to-peer, smart grids, computational grids, data centers networking), leverage and advance new networking technologies; Future Internet Architecture – Next Phase (demonstrate prototype systems, security); GENI (WiFi, WiMAX, deploy GENI racks); NSF Cloud program (infrastructure, academic/industry interaction); Campus Cyberinfrastructure- Infrastructure, Innovation and Engineering program ([CC*IIE] end-to-end access to dynamic network services, support for innovative networking); International Research Connections program ([IRNC], international multi-Gbps, SDN-based experiments, >200 Gbps trans-Atlantic connectivity); Cyberinfrastructure for 21st Century Science and Engineering ([CIF21] integrated scalable cyberinfrastructure across all science and engineering disciplines); Cyber-Enabled Sustainability Science and Engineering ([CyberSEES] sustainability research, energy efficient, disaster resilient)

- **ONR**: Spectrum and energy efficient communications; tactical communications (high bandwidth optical and wireless, dynamic spectrum access, underwater links for sensors); underwater communications (mobility-driven architecture, DTN, increased bandwidth); dynamic tactical communications networks; control of heterogeneous wireless networks, cross-layer network control

Social, Economic, and Workforce Implications of IT and IT Workforce Development (SEW)

NITRD Agencies: AFOSR, ARO, DARPA, DHS, DOE/NNSA, NASA, NIH, NIST, NSF, NRL, ONR, and OSD
Other Participants: BLS, ED, IARPA, and USDA

Research activities funded under the SEW PCA focus on the co-evolution of IT and social, economic, and workforce systems, including interactions between people and IT and among people developing and using IT in groups, organizations, and larger social networks. Collaborative science concerns are addressed including improving the effectiveness of teams and enhancing geographically distributed, interdisciplinary R&D to engage societal concerns, such as competitiveness, security, economic development, and wellbeing. Workforce concerns are addressed by leveraging interagency efforts to improve education outcomes through the use of learning technologies that anticipate the educational needs of individuals and society. SEW also supports efforts to speed the transfer of R&D results to the policymaker, practitioner, and IT user communities in all sectors.

President's FY 2015 Request

Strategic Priorities Underlying This Request

Priorities in SEW reflect the sweeping socio-technical transformations occurring as a result of 21st century life in an increasingly networked society. From crowdsourcing to e-science to cyberlearning, new forms of social collaboration and problem-solving increasingly leverage networked, online environments. In cyberspace, thousands voluntarily contribute time and intellectual resources for collective tasks, such as writing open-source software, classifying galaxies, and identifying words in non-machine-readable text. Global multidisciplinary teams connected through cyberinfrastructure play a central role in addressing societal needs, such as developing economical solar power, mitigating environmental disasters, delivering new medical interventions, and maintaining our national security. A new era of human-machine partnerships is emerging, but we do not yet understand how to harness these novel forms of collective action most effectively. In this new era, developing cyber-capable citizens is also critical – from the ability to use digital capabilities wisely and effectively, to the IT skills and knowledge needed in the advanced technical workforce of tomorrow. It is imperative that the general population be able to understand the challenges in complex systems, such as in healthcare information infrastructures, e-commerce, and cyberlearning, and to balance trade-offs with respect to privacy, security, and reliability. SEW priorities exemplify the scope of these concerns among the NITRD agencies. Many SEW activities involve extending understanding and applications of IT to help people learn, conduct research, and innovate more effectively. Key focus areas include:

- **Collaboration**
    - **Increase fundamental knowledge**: To better understand how to efficiently and effectively manage, conduct, fund, and support science teams collaborating with and via cyberinfrastructure by developing evidence-based approaches for managing, conducting, funding, and evaluating effective and efficient cross-disciplinary collaborative research

    - **Integrated multidisciplinary research**: Support research, development, and education that address societal challenges using a multidisciplinary systems-based approach to understand, predict, and react to changes in the linked natural, social, and built environment – especially in climate change, energy, health, education, and security

    - **Research networking and profiling tools**: Advance our understanding of the complex and increasingly coupled nature of scientific research to facilitate collaboration among Federal agencies and to increase the cross-fertilization of ideas and collaborative effectiveness and efficiency within and across agencies

- **Education**

- o **Transform science teaching across educational settings**: Integrate STEM education R&D and IT innovations to improve learning in science and engineering disciplines. Bring new evidence-based practices, content, knowledge, and real-world applications to more learners. Provide evidence-based professional development and support to STEM educators in the classroom to improve STEM instruction and retain effective teachers

- o **Cyberlearning**: Promote understanding and support for effective IT-enabled learning in all educational settings to enhance learning anytime in any location. Provide learning that is personalized and tailored to the needs of diverse learners. Transform science teaching across educational settings

- o **Computational competencies for everyone**: Explore how the nature and meaning of computational competence can be incorporated into K-12, informal, and higher education

- o **IT education and training**: Develop innovative approaches to broaden interest and participation in 21st century IT careers, including information assurance and computer security

- o **Preparing effective STEM teachers**: Recruit, prepare, and support talented individuals with strong content knowledge to become effective STEM teachers; engage STEM teachers in influencing the design and development of educational technologies (EdTech) and in understanding evidence on learning styles to use to teach effectively in IT-enabled learning settings that span beyond the classroom

- **Social computing**

  - o **Increase fundamental knowledge**: The recently formed NITRD Social Computing Team is focusing on understanding the wide range of systems that support interactions among large numbers of individuals at different scales, but differ along a number of dimensions: the topology and goals of interaction, media richness, and degree of virtualness. Research is needed to understand how to design such systems and make them effective, rewarding, and sustainable; to understand the dynamics of online social systems; and to understand the technical effects that emerging social phenomena empowered by ubiquitous online services have on specific areas such as security, privacy, health, and scientific discovery

Highlights of the Request

The SEW agencies report the following topical areas as highlights of their planned R&D investments for FY 2015. Agencies are listed in alphabetical order:

- **Collaboration**

  - o **Multidisciplinary centers, institutes, and communities**: Support collaborative activities to advance a field or create new directions in research or education by enabling coordination of research, training, and educational activities across disciplinary, organizational, geographic, and international boundaries. Create centers to coordinate multiyear activities addressing national challenges such as big data, translational sciences, energy efficiency, environmental sustainability, advanced communication, transportation, learning, and healthcare systems – DOE/NNSA, NASA, NIH, and NSF

  - o **Cyber-human systems**: Focus on the co-evolution of social and technical systems to create new knowledge about human-machine partnerships and of the purposeful design of such systems, including e-science collaboration tools, human-robot partnerships, cyber-physical systems, advanced manufacturing, cyber-enabled materials, manufacturing and smart systems, and handling big data – NASA, NIH, and NSF

  - o **Improving health and wellbeing**: Leverage the scientific methods and knowledge bases of a broad range of computing and communication research perspectives to facilitate long-term, transformative change in how we treat illness and maintain our health; improve safe, effective, efficient, equitable, and patient-centered health and wellness services – NIH and NSF

- o **Sustainability science, engineering, and education**: Generate the discoveries and capabilities in climate and energy science and engineering needed to inform societal actions that lead to environmental and economic sustainability; support interdisciplinary communities focused on sustainability science – NSF

- **Education**

  - o **Advanced learning technologies**: Understand advanced learning technologies that have demonstrated potential to transform STEM teaching and learning at all levels across all societal settings; understand technologies that can contribute to a highly interdisciplinary technical STEM workforce; enable new avenues of STEM learning with novel, collaborative, and global learning experiences for students, the general public, and the emerging IT workforce; advance the Nation's ability to study the learning process discretely and rapidly deploy new understandings and adaptive and assistive resources in education to broaden participation of all Americans in STEM R&D, including returning disabled veterans – ED, NSF and ONR

  - o **Cybersecurity education**: Bolster formal education programs to focus on cybersecurity and STEM – ED, NIST, and NSF

  - o **Cybersecurity workforce training and professional development**: Intensify training and professional development programs for the existing cybersecurity workforce – DARPA, DHS, DoD, NIST, and other agencies

- **Social computing**

  - o **Social computing**: Collect information about existing Social Computing programs and initiatives across Federal agencies to determine if there are overlaps and collaboration opportunities and to identify gaps for multiagency R&D funding – DARPA, NSF, and other agencies

Planning and Coordination Supporting Request

The SEW Coordinating Group (SEW CG) continues to pursue opportunities for expanded interagency collaborations to improve IT education and workforce training, team science, and social computing. Over the coming year, the SEW CG plans to engage in a series of workshop discussions to develop strategic plans and associated agendas for its three teams: SEW-Collaboration, SEW-Education, and Social Computing. The SEW CG also promotes interactions between IT researchers, practitioners, and government policymakers. The SEW-Collab Team plans to engage agencies in developing best practices for planning and evaluating large collaborative proposals. The SEW-Ed Team continues to track the proposed reorganization of Federal Science, Technology, Engineering, and Mathematics (STEM) Education programs, as outlined in the Federal STEM Education 5-Year Strategic Plan.[13] The Plan identifies NSF, ED, and the Smithsonian Institution as the lead agencies for Federal STEM education programs. This past year the SEW CG established the Social Computing Team in response to a recommendation of the PCAST to develop a coordinated cross-agency initiative in social computing. In the upcoming year, the Social Computing Team plans to focus on and coordinate efforts that emphasize crisis management, crowdsourcing, cognitive security, and social sensors.

Additional 2014 and 2015 Activities by Agency

The following list provides a summary of individual agencies' ongoing programmatic interests for 2014 and 2015 under the SEW PCA:

- **DoD**: Meet the DoD's requirements for a diverse, world-class STEM talent pool with the creativity and agility to meet national defense needs; ensure the implementation of the DoD STEM Strategic Plan aligns with the

---

[13] *Federal Science, Technology, Engineering, and Mathematics (STEM) Education 5-Year Strategic Plan*, May 2013, NSTC: http://www.whitehouse.gov/sites/default/files/microsites/ostp/stem_stratplan_2013.pdf

DoD's Strategic Workforce Plan and the NSTC Committee on STEM Education 5-Year Strategic Plan; assess and leverage DoD STEM investments

- **DOE/NNSA**: Critical-skills development program for university participants in the Advanced Simulation and Computing (ASC) Alliance Program

- **NIH (NCI, NLM)**: Promote the use of technologies that improve educational outcomes of both trainees and established scientists by facilitating the efficient acquisition of knowledge and skills. Increase knowledge of scientific workforce dynamics in areas critical to advancing the NIH mission by developing evidence-informed policy decisions (NIGMS grants)

- **NIST**: Designated lead agency for the National Initiative for Cybersecurity Education (NICE) to promote coordination of existing and future activities in cybersecurity education, training, and awareness to strengthen the overall cybersecurity posture of the U.S. by accelerating the availability of educational and training resources designed to improve cybersecurity behavior, skills, and knowledge

- **NSF**: Advance new modes of collective intelligence (e.g., social, participatory, and intelligent computing) while also ensuring that human values are embedded in these emerging systems and infrastructures; support the human capital essential for advances across all disciplines by linking key areas of educational investments in HEC, data, education, software, virtual organizations, networking, and campus bridging; Transformative Computational Science using CyberInstrastructure (CI TraCS) effort to support outstanding scientists and engineers who have recently completed doctoral studies and are interested in pursuing postdoctoral activities in computational science; broaden participation in computing by underrepresented minorities; support faculty, graduate, and undergraduate fellowships, traineeships, and junior faculty; promote digital gaming in education; Discovery Research K-12 (DRK-12) program for significant and sustainable improvements in STEM learning, advance STEM teaching, and contribute to improvements in the Nation's formal education system

- **ONR**: The Information Dominance and Cybersecurity program seeks to advance the science of security through interdisciplinary research to ensure safe and secure operations in cyberspace; the Naval Research Enterprise Summer Intern Program (NREIP) allows students to participate in naval research; Mission Ocean allows fifth-through eighth-grade level students to gain hands-on experience operating a simulated submarine; and the SeaPerch Program provides students with the opportunity to learn about robotics, engineering, science, and mathematics while building an underwater remotely operated vehicle (ROV) as part of a science and engineering curriculum; Technovation Challenge allows high school-aged entrepreneurial young women to pair with a female near-peer mentor for a team App development competition working with venture capitalists who develop and release the winning App; National Junior Science and Humanities Symposia (JSHS) jointly funded by Army, Navy, and Air Force to promote original research and experimentation in science, engineering, and mathematics at the high school level

Software Design and Productivity (SDP)

NITRD Agencies: AFRL, DARPA, DHS, DOE/SC, NASA, NIH, NIST, NOAA, NSF, ONR, and OSD
Other Participants: FAA, FDA, and NRC

A computational revolution is transforming industry and society, driven by software operating and interacting with physical, personal, and social environments. Software and the possibilities for computational behaviors are transforming every facet of every industry. Products that are not computational are dependent upon computationally intensive simulation-based engineering and science (SBE&S) or manufactured by computational machinery. Pervasive computational behaviors present enormous opportunities for industry and society but also pose significant challenges. Current technology works quite well in many familiar domains of modest scale, so long as the error-prone characteristic of the software is accepted. However the world is changing in a big way (e.g., autonomy, biocomputing, multicores, social networking, big data, thought-driven prosthetics, programmable matter) and current software technology is not advancing sufficiently to keep up. Meeting these challenges requires solving the intellectually deep, difficult, and important problems in the science, mathematics, and engineering of computational behaviors, information processes, and software representations.

The SDP R&D agenda spans the science and the technology of software creation and sustainment (e.g., development methods and environments, V&V technologies, component technologies, languages, and tools) and software project management in diverse domains. R&D will advance software engineering concepts, methods, techniques, and tools that result in more usable, dependable, cost-effective, evolvable, and sustainable software-intensive systems. The domains cut across information technology, industrial production, evolving areas such as the Internet, and highly complex, interconnected software-intensive systems. The core SDP R&D activities are software productivity, software cost, responsiveness to change, and sustainment. The success of these activities can have a major beneficial effect on high-confidence systems because such systems are critically dependent upon the quality of the software and on the many companies producing software-reliant products.

President's FY 2015 Request

Strategic Priorities Underlying This Request

Complex software-based systems today power the Nation's most advanced defense, security, and economic capabilities. Such systems also play central roles in science and engineering discovery and, thus, are essential in addressing this century's grand challenges (e.g., low-cost, carbon-neutral, and renewable energy; clean water; next-generation health care; extreme manufacturing; space exploration, etc.). These large-scale systems typically must remain operational, useful, and relevant for decades. The involved agencies are working to identify and define the core elements for a new science of software development that will make engineering decisions and modifications transparent and traceable throughout the software lifecycle (e.g., design, development, evolution, and sustainment). A key goal of this science framework is to enable software engineers to maintain and evolve complex systems cost-effectively and correctly long after the original developers have departed. This new science of software development will also benefit the many companies producing software-reliant products that comprise an increasing portion of the economy. The following areas are research priorities:

- **Research to rethink software design**: From the basic concepts of design, evolution, and adaptation to advanced systems that seamlessly integrate human and computational capabilities, including:

  - **Foundational/core research on science and engineering of software:** Develop new computational models and logics, techniques, languages, tools, metrics, and processes for developing and analyzing software for complex software-intensive systems (e.g., a fundamental approach to software engineering that can provide systems that are verifiably correct, assured, efficient, effective, reliable, and sustainable)

- o **Next-generation software concepts, methods, and tools:** Reformulation of the development process, the tool chain, the partitioning of tasks and resources; open technology development (open-source and open-systems methods); technology from nontraditional sources; multidisciplinary and crosscutting concepts and approaches; and next-generation software concepts, methods, and tools will be needed for emerging technologies such as multicore, software-as-a-service, cloud computing, end-user programming, quantum information processing; and modeling of human-machine systems

  - o **Capabilities for building evolvable, sustainable, long-lived software-intensive systems:** Exploration of new means to create, keep current, and use engineering artifacts to support long-lived software-intensive systems; new approaches to reliably meet changing requirements and assure security and safety; and long-term retention and archiving of software-development data and institutional knowledge

- **Explore fundamental principles:** Understand, design, analyze, and build software systems that are verifiable, regardless of size, scale, complexity, and heterogeneity, and are correct, assured, efficient, effective, and predictable. Build foundations of software for emerging quantum information science and quantum information processing

- **Develop predictable, timely, cost-effective software-intensive systems**: Disciplined methods, technologies, and tools for systems and software engineering, rapidly evaluating alternative solutions to address evolving needs; measuring, predicting, and controlling software properties and tradeoffs; virtualized and model-based development environments; automation of deterministic engineering tasks; and scalable analysis, test generation, optimization, and verification with traceability to requirements; related issues include:

  - o **Software application interoperability and usability**: Develop interface and integration standards, representation methods to enable software interoperability, data exchanges, interoperable databases; supply-chain system integration; and standardized software engineering practices for model development

  - o **Cost and productivity issues in development of safety-critical, embedded, and autonomous systems**: Research on composition, reuse, power tools, training, and education to address systems that can be inaccessible after deployment (e.g., spacecraft) and need to operate autonomously

- **Transform SDP frontiers:** Invest in challenging, potentially transformative research; prepare and engage a diverse STEM workforce; sharpen the merit-review process to better identify such research; emphasize interdisciplinary and system-oriented approaches that can lead to transformational concepts

- **Improve health IT interoperability:** Improve conformance testing, testability, and community knowledge of specifications

- **Advance supply chain interoperability for digital manufacturing research**: Use model-based engineering, product manufacturing information standards, and systems engineering standards

- **Assess software quality**: Provide reference datasets and test programs for software assurance and metrics

- **Focus on Smart Grid security guidelines**: Support the multidisciplinary aspects of Smart Grid security

Highlights of the Request

The SDP agencies report the following topical areas as highlights of their planned R&D investments for FY 2015. Agencies are listed in alphabetical order:

- **Software Infrastructure for Sustained Innovation (SI^2):** Agency-wide program for development and integration of next-generation software infrastructure to advance scientific discovery and education at all levels in the sciences, mathematics, and engineering – NSF

- **Cyberinfrastructure Framework for 21st Century Science and Engineering (CIF21)**: Development of new algorithms, tools, and other applications to support innovation – NSF

- **Software and hardware foundations**: Scientific and engineering principles and new logics, languages, architectures, and tools for specifying, designing, programming, analyzing, and verifying software and software-intensive systems; V&V tools for sound development of reliable and assured software; formal definitions of weaknesses; standards for certification; and techniques that enable prediction of cost and schedule for large-scale software projects – AFOSR, AFRL, NASA, NIST, NOAA, NSF, ONR, and OSD

- **Computer systems research**: Rethink and transform the software stack for computer systems in different application domains (e.g., new reference architectures for embedded systems); investigate systems that involve computational, human/social, and physical elements – AFOSR, AFRL, NASA, NIST, NSF, ONR, and OSD

- **Intelligent software design**: Investigate approaches to design software-intensive systems that operate in complex, real-time, distributed, and unpredictable environments; invariant refinement of software properties; automation and scaling of testing, validation, and system-level verification; automated analysis of model-based software development; transformational approaches to drastically reduce software life-cycle costs, complexity, and to extend life span; languages and modeling tools that support interoperability, data exchange among engineering tools, large-scale simulations, and federated information systems – AFOSR, DARPA, NASA, NIST, NOAA, NSF, ONR, and OSD

- **Interoperability standards, knowledge capture processes**: Develop representation schemes for interoperability among computer-aided engineering systems; standards for instrument, mathematical, and measurement data; ontological approaches to facilitate integrating supply-chain systems; interoperability of databases; interoperability testing tools – NIST; and infrastructure for capture, reuse of domain expertise – NOAA, ONR, and OSD

- **Cyber-Enabled Materials, Manufacturing, and Smart Systems (CEMMSS)**: Enable smart systems technology framework for advanced manufacturing to establish a scientific basis for engineered systems interdependent with the physical world and social systems; synthesize multidisciplinary knowledge to model and simulate systems in their full complexity and dynamics; this framework expands cyber-physical systems and includes investments in the National Robotics Initiative (NRI), a multiagency activity – NSF

- **Science, Engineering, and Education for Sustainability (SEES)**: Explore the role of software in a sustainable energy future to advance science, engineering, and education to inform the societal actions needed for environmental and economic sustainability and sustainable human wellbeing – NSF

- **Quantum Information Sciences**: Support Federal S&T Quantum Information Sciences IWG – NIST

Planning and Coordination Supporting Request

The SDP agencies' current collaboration activities focus on domain areas in which large-scale, software-intensive, and cyber-physical systems predominate – such as in aviation, air-traffic control, and global climate and weather modeling – and on building a forward-looking research agenda to improve the engineering and evolution of such systems. NITRD agencies sponsor workshops to ensure collaboration among the government, industry, and academia (e.g., NSF CPS PI, NSF Secure and Trustworthy Cyberspace (SaTC) PI, and NITRD SDP national needs, opportunities, and priorities workshops).

- **Software verification and validation**: Ongoing collaboration to develop effective approaches for next-generation air transportation – FAA and NASA

- **Articulate SDP national needs, opportunities, and priorities:** Provide a focus for the future of software engineering research, and discuss and formulate software and productivity research goals and priorities – SDP agencies

- **Earth System Modeling Framework (ESMF), weather research, and forecasting**: Long-term multiagency efforts to build, use common software toolset, data standards; visualization for weather and climate applications – DoD Service research organizations, DOE/SC, NASA, NOAA, and NSF

- **Automatic program and processor synthesis for data dependent applications:** From high-level mathematical description, generate code with performance comparable to hand-written code – ONR

- **Automated combinatorial testing of software systems**: Methodology and infrastructure for automated testing that reduces the number of tests – NASA and NIST

- **Next-generation aircraft**: Collaboration on concepts, modeling and simulation tools – DoD Service research organizations, FAA, and NASA

Additional 2014 and 2015 Activities by Agency

The following list provides a summary of individual agencies' ongoing programmatic interests for 2014 and 2015 under the SDP PCA:

- **AFRL**: Research in new methods, tools for developing reliable, sustainable software-intensive systems for complex real-world environments with human-machine interactions; focus areas include model-based analysis and synthesis, modeling of human-machine interaction, advanced algorithms for real-time and distributed systems, language-based assurance, and formal analysis and verification

- **DARPA**: Apply formal methods to mission critical applications; create web-based techniques to support large-scale formal software verification workflows; develop automated program analysis techniques for mathematically validating the security properties of mobile applications; develop program analyses and frameworks for improving the resilience and reliability of large-scale and data-intensive computations

- **NASA**: Architecture for SensorWeb for Earth sciences; integrated vehicle health management tools and techniques to enable automated detection, diagnosis, prognosis, and mitigation of adverse events during flight; integrated aircraft control design tools and techniques; and physics-based Multidisciplinary Analysis Optimization (MDAO) framework for cost-effective advanced modeling in development of next-generation aircraft and spacecraft

- **NIST**: Standards development and testing tools supporting interoperability such as schema validation, semantics, automated test generation (conformance testing), naming and design rules; product data models and modeling tools; methods to facilitate 3D shape search; Units Markup Language; precisely and accurately define classes of software weaknesses which will serve as a basis for tool interoperability and proofs that a tool or technique precludes certain classes of weaknesses; run SATE to understand the contribution of such tools to assurance; and convene Software Testing Metrics and Standards workshop to document state of the art in testing and to map gaps and needed research; tools and metrics to support better quality software and software testing and to support innovation in software-dependent industries

- **NOAA**: Standard and consistent software development practices for environmental modeling; continue adoption of ESMF as part of overall modeling activities; and computer science aspects of software development, including collaboration with universities on programming model for fine-grain parallel architectures

- **NSF**: Advance core research on the science and engineering of software development and evolution, including formal mathematical/logical foundations and automated development methods, programming languages and methodologies, software testing and analysis, empirical software research, and human-centered computing; coordinate SDP-related areas (e.g., productivity, cost, responsiveness of software, and evolution) in crosscutting topics and programs, including SI^2, SaTC, and effective software design for real-world systems in healthcare, manufacturing, etc.; SEES research on software advances to meet energy requirements in computation and communication; and programmability with assurance underlying key domains such as HPC, health IT, robotics, nanotechnology, and cyber-physical systems

- **ONR**: Automated generation of secure and robust codes from high-level description (design-entry) of functions that lead to software that is both readable and efficient; to methods that automatically capture and use work flow, thought/design-decision documentation during development and sustainment and leads to implementations that meet performance and security requirements; to technologies for real-time control of distributed and embedded systems; to methods for intelligent orchestration of Web services; to language and system for building secure, federated, distributed information systems; to analysis tools for modeling, testing software component interactions; to software for quantum processing; to automated software de-bloating and de-layering to reduce software complexity, size/attack-surface, and achieve highly efficient, compact, secure programs; and to develop novel architectures and protocols for real-time control of embedded sensors, new reference architectures for embedded systems, and promote reusability

- **OSD**: SDP research is a critical part of the overall DoD software assurance posture. OSD's primary effort in SDP is in the research program at the Software Engineering Institute (SEI) Federally Funded Research and Development Center (FFRDC). The program addresses composability and timing at all scales, computing for real-time and embedded systems, multicore programming, computing at the tactical edge, and system of system architectures. The OSD Software Producibility Initiative addresses tools and techniques to improve the efficiency of software production across the DoD. The initiative includes correct-by-construction methods, model-driven development, validation and verification of complex systems (greater than 20 million lines of code), software visualization, static and dynamic analysis, deterministic behavior in software, interoperable multiscale and multidomain models, and efficient execution of distributed and multicore processing

Additional Program Focus Areas

Big Data R&D (BD)

Participating Agencies: DARPA, DoD Service Research Organizations, DOE/NNSA, DOE/SC, EPA, NASA, NIH, NIST, NOAA, NRO, NSA, NSF, OSD, Treasury/OFR, USAID, and USGS

The Big Data Senior Steering Group (BD SSG) was formed in early 2011 to identify current big data research and development activities across the Federal Government; offer opportunities for coordination among agencies, academia, and the private sector; and help establish the goals for a National Big Data R&D Initiative. After a successful multiagency launch in 2012, the focus over the past year has been to encourage multiple stakeholders, including Federal agencies, private industry, academia, state and local governments, non-profits, and foundations, to develop and participate in big data innovation projects across the country; highlight high-impact collaborations; and identify areas for expanded collaboration between the public and private sectors. There is a recognition that all sectors of the innovation ecosystem need to be actively involved to help achieve the advantages of big data.

Strategic Priorities

The BD SSG envisions a future in which the ability to analyze and extract knowledge and insights from large, diverse, and disparate data sets will accelerate the progress of scientific discovery and innovation; promote new economic growth; and lead to new fields of research and new areas of inquiry that would otherwise not be possible. The BD SSG strategic priorities include:

- Education and workforce development

- Research and innovation

- Cyberinfrastructure, including data archives, data interoperability, data forensics, and crosscutting data analytics

- Community engagement and outreach

Current and Planned Coordination Activities

The current and planned coordination activities of the BD SSG include:

- *White House Big Data events*: In conjunction with the White House Office of Science and Technology Policy, the BD SSG held the "Big Data Partners Workshop" on May 3, 2013 and the "Data to Knowledge to Action" event on November 12, 2013. Between the two events, over 30 multi-sector partnerships were identified and highlighted, demos were staged, and six community discussion sessions were offered on topics such as partnerships for innovation, public engagement, education and workforce development, and research and development

- *Joint NSF-NIH solicitation*: Under the joint NSF-NIH solicitation, "Core Techniques and Technologies for Advancing Big Data Science & Engineering," the mid-scale competition (up to $650K/year for 5 years) reviewed 136 proposals and made 11 awards totaling $20M, and the small-scale competition (up to $150K/year for 3 years) reviewed 350 proposals and made 34 awards totaling $24M. NSF will be re-issuing a similarly scoped solicitation in 2014

- *Workforce training*: To address the lack of a sufficiently trained workforce, the BD SSG participated in the 2013 Joint Statistical Meeting by hosting the session "Big Data: Curriculum Development and Funding Opportunities." NSF funded the National Academies to hold a workshop in 2014 on Big Data Education and Workforce Development, while NIH has new training opportunities in 2014 through its Big Data to Knowledge (BD2K) initiative

- *Workshop on data sharing and metadata issues*: The "Data Sharing and Metadata Curation: Obstacles and Strategies" workshop, held on May 29, 2013, brought together experts from different perspectives across a variety of domains to discuss interoperability and metadata issues and solutions pertaining to big data

- *Ideation challenges*: There were three separate ideation challenges; one focused on big data fusion and creating homogeneous data sets from heterogeneous sources across domains, and the other two focused on big data topical tracks in energy and earth science. The next set of challenges is currently under discussion

Cyber-Physical Systems R&D (CPS)

Participating Agencies: DARPA, DHS, DoD Service Research Organizations, DOE, DOT, FDA, NASA, NIH, NIST, NSA, NSF, OSD, and USDA

The Cyber Physical Systems Senior Steering Group (CPS SSG) was established in 2012 in response to an ongoing effort by NITRD agencies to foster a multidisciplinary research agenda to develop the next-generation of engineered systems—systems that depend on ubiquitous cyber control and require very high levels of system assurance. Establishing the CPS SSG was additionally in response to a recommendation of the PCAST for NITRD to coordinate a focused research effort on NIT-enabled interaction with the physical world.

Cyber-physical systems (CPS) are smart networked systems with embedded sensors, processors, and actuators that are designed to sense and interact with the physical world (including human users), and support real-time, guaranteed performance in safety-critical applications. In CPS systems, the joint behavior of the "cyber" and "physical" elements of the system is critical—computing, control, sensing, and networking are deeply integrated into every component, and the actions of components and systems must be carefully orchestrated.

Strategic Priorities

The CPS SSG has developed a vision statement[14] that identifies the following sectors as strategic priorities for research and development. Because CPS technologies are affecting these sectors already, there is the potential for high impact, crosscutting results and for advancing a common body of knowledge in CPS technologies.

- *Transportation*: Improve efficiency and safety in transportation. Reduce human errors in vehicles and reduce highway congestion; reduce congestion at airports and the rate of runway incursions

- *Manufacturing*: Preserve competitiveness in manufacturing and protect national security. CPS technologies are vital as products' complexity and variety increase while time-to-market decreases

- *Healthcare*: Design cost-effective, easy-to-certify, and safe products using CPS correct-by-construction design methodologies. Healthcare demands will lead to growth in cyber-physical medical products

- *Energy*: Develop the smart infrastructure to enable the optimization and management of resources and facilities and allow consumers to control and manage their energy consumption

- *Agriculture*: Increase efficiency between production and consumption; improve our environmental footprint. Develop high-skill workforce opportunities and sustainable practices, processes, and systems

- *Defense*: Improve CPS science and technology in complex, networked systems to meet military and national defense needs, especially in engineering resilient systems, cyberspace operations, and autonomous systems

- *Emergency response*: Increase situational awareness and optimize the response of emergency responders through all phases of disaster events such as earthquakes, hurricanes, and man-made disasters

- *Society*: Invest in basic research. "Apps" that network with the physical world are becoming common; consumers want tasks automated and interoperable devices. Commercialization will repay investments

The CPS SSG also identified four crosscutting strategic challenges that are essential to success in all the sectors:

- *Cybersecurity*: Build resilience to cyber-attacks to ensure safety, wellbeing, and economic stability. Attacks made on the financial system, intelligence databases, and e-commerce sites could be replicated with serious consequences to networked, cyber-physical systems and critical infrastructure such as the Smart Grid, biomedical systems, and transportation networks

---

[14] Cyber Physical Systems Vision Statement: http://www.nitrd.gov/nitrdgroups/images/6/6a/Cyber_Physical_Systems_%28CPS%29_Vision_Statement.pdf

- *Privacy*: Develop mechanisms, policies, and techniques that enable the appropriate use of sensitive and personal information while protecting personal privacy in the context of CPS systems

- *Economics*: Improve open reference architectures and standards, model-based engineering methodologies, and powerful simulation, verification, and validation tools to reduce the cost of developing CPS systems

- *Interoperability*: Enhance capabilities for assembling individual CPSs into interacting systems of systems

Current and Planned Coordination Activities

The CPS SSG is pursuing a multiagency, multi-sector, comprehensive focus on crosscutting R&D challenges to address gaps in the Federal CPS R&D portfolio. A concerted effort is necessary to break through the many technical barriers that arise throughout the stages of technology development, from basic science through applied R&D, and that impede the rapid, predictable development and deployment of CPS systems. There are also natural synergies from which to learn and advance foundational knowledge. For example, there are natural synergies between designing secure, but easy-to-monitor, reprogrammable, networked medical devices and developing services for the Smart Grid that allow operators to adapt to changing conditions while ensuring safety. In line with a synergistic approach, the current and planned coordination activities of the CPS SSG include:

- *Partnerships for innovation*: Address R&D gaps through close collaborations among industry, academia, and government contributors. Each agency, consistent with its mission authorities, will develop models for the strategic management of intellectual property rights and will include education and training in the mix of engineering and computer science skills that are critical to CPS

- *Mechanisms for cooperation*: In keeping with agencies' diverse capabilities and communities, there will be a spectrum of mechanisms to facilitate agency cooperation. These include:

  o Participating in the CPS SSG as a representative of a funding agency

  o Being involved in a reporting requirement activity, e.g., common PI meetings or workshops

  o Extending funding opportunities to others, e.g., an agency funding a project could grant access to proposals to allow for supplementary funding by another agency

  o Broadening the mix of funding options, e.g., joint or coordinated solicitations might include a mix of intramural and extramural funding

- *Mechanisms for funding*: There is a range of possible funding mechanisms, from a tightly coupled mechanism (joint solicitation) to a loosely coupled mechanism (independent solicitations with collaborative research) that might include a mix of intramural and extramural funding:

  o *Joint solicitations*: Advertise joint solicitations with topics of interest to multiple funding agencies

  o *Coordinated solicitations*: Coordinate solicitations to ensure there are no R&D gaps or overlaps

  o *Independent solicitations with collaborative research*: Identify synergistic research projects in independent solicitations that enable PIs funded by one agency to collaborate with PIs funded by another agency

Cybersecurity and Information Assurance R&D (CSIA R&D)

Participating Agencies: DHS, NIST, NSA, NSF, ODNI, and OSD

The Cybersecurity and Information Assurance R&D Senior Steering Group (CSIA R&D SSG) was formed in response to the January 2008 Comprehensive National Cybersecurity Initiative (CNCI) – National Security Presidential Directive 54/Homeland Security Presidential Directive 23. This initiative called for the Director of the Office of Science and Technology Policy to "develop a detailed plan to coordinate classified and unclassified cyber research." The purpose of the CSIA R&D SSG is to provide overall leadership for cybersecurity research and development coordination, and to streamline decision processes to support evolving research and budget priorities. The CSIA R&D SSG is composed of senior representatives of agencies with national cybersecurity leadership positions.

Strategic Priorities

The CSIA R&D SSG seeks principally to streamline the communication between research planning among agencies' technical managers and budgetary decision making to accelerate advances in transformative research and deployable technologies. The CSIA R&D SSG is therefore positioned to communicate research needs and proposed budget priorities to policy makers and budget officials. Similarly, the CSIA R&D SSG relays priorities and other pertinent information from higher Federal policy levels to inform research and development coordination activities. The CSIA R&D SSG's strategic priorities include:

- Prioritizing Federal cybersecurity research and development areas and ensuring that the entire spectrum of research and development priorities and key technology challenges across the Federal Government are being addressed

- Leading strategic research and development coordination efforts in addressing Administration priorities

- Formulating and evolving a framework for research and development strategies that focuses on game-changing technologies

Current and Planned Coordination Activities

The CSIA R&D SSG planned activities include:

- Coordinating research and development objectives and the allocation of Federal budgets to support them

- Developing and sponsoring events to advance the national research agenda necessary to fulfill key objectives of the Federal cybersecurity R&D strategic plan

- Promoting effective Federal cybersecurity research and development coordination among government agencies and with academia and industry by prioritizing research needs and determining appropriate investment strategies, enabling broad multidisciplinary and multi-sector efforts, enabling agencies to leverage resources, and improving synergy between classified and unclassified Federal research

- Exploring the strategic plan's research themes and how they can drive better security solutions in sectors such as the Smart Grid, health IT, and transportation

- Cultivating and supporting a research community in the area of the science of security

- Developing focused activities to help accelerate the transition of research into practice

- Coordinating and promoting activities leading to effective education programs and career options in cybersecurity

- Examining opportunities to coordinate and strengthen research activities supporting privacy in cyberspace

Health Information Technology R&D (HITRD)

Participating Agencies: AHRQ, ASPR, CDC, CMS, DoD, FDA, IHS, NIH, NIST, NSF, ONC, and VA

The Health Information Technology R&D Senior Steering Group (HITRD SSG) was established in the fall of 2010 in response to Section 13202(b) of the American Recovery and Reinvestment Act of 2009 (ARRA, P.L. 111-5), which directed the NITRD Program to include Federal research and development programs related to health information technology.

HITRD SSG participants are working collaboratively to articulate health IT R&D needs for policy and decision makers, and to capitalize on interagency opportunities to advance IT research, innovation, and interoperable health IT systems.

Strategic Priorities

The HITRD SSG coordinates interagency information sharing for health IT R&D planning to promote synergies across Federal health IT investments and to advance IT research for use in healthcare delivery, disease management, disaster and emergency preparedness and response, and lifelong health and wellness. The strategic priorities of the HITRD SSG include:

- Addressing multiagency leadership in health IT interoperability and the development of innovative applications

- Bringing together the health IT and information technology R&D communities to focus on health IT research and development needs

- Enhancing synergies across agencies' complementary health IT research interests

Current and Planned Coordination Activities

The current and planned coordination activities of the HITRD SSG include:

- *Strategic Planning*: Coordinating with ONC on the update to the *Federal Health Information Technology Strategic Plan 2011-2015*. ONC is working with the HITRD SSG and Federal agency partners to update and publish the 2014-2018 edition of the Strategic Plan by the end of 2014

- *Research Gaps*: Analyzing IT R&D gaps related to electronic health records, evidence-based decision support, standards and interoperability, privacy and security, modeling and simulation, data analytics, natural language processing, semantic technologies, knowledge repositories and metadata usage, public health surveillance, patient safety, clinical quality measures, clinical trials, personalized medicine, usability, image quality, mobile health and wireless sensors, assistive and medical devices, consumer health IT, and other IT of potential benefit to health and healthcare

- *Health IT R&D Needs*: Assessing health IT research and development needs against the shifting landscape of today's healthcare system and the profound transformation that the system is undergoing due, in part, to widespread adoption of health IT, changes in care payment models, the influx of consumer and business intelligence IT to healthcare settings (for example, mobile devices, social computing, and big data analytics), emerging information technologies (such as body area networks), and major scientific breakthroughs in understanding the role of the genome in health and disease

Wireless Spectrum R&D (WSRD)

Participating Agencies: DARPA, DHS, DoD Service Research Organizations, DOJ/NIJ, FAA, FCC, NASA, NIST, NSA, NSF, NTIA, and OSD

The Wireless Spectrum R&D Senior Steering Group (WSRD SSG) was established in 2010 in response to the June 28, 2010 *Presidential Memorandum – Unleashing the Wireless Broadband Revolution.*[15] NITRD is supporting the Secretary of Commerce, through NTIA, in consultation with NIST, NSF, DoD, DOJ, NASA, and other agencies, to facilitate research, development, experimentation, and testing by researchers to explore innovative spectrum-sharing technologies.

Strategic Priorities

WSRD SSG member agencies have been funding research and development to enable more efficient use of the radio spectrum through spectrum-sharing technologies. Working within the requirements of the Presidential Memorandum and with guidance from the President's Chief Technology Officer, the WSRD SSG has held a series of workshops to gather information from academic and private sector researchers to help maximize the efforts to increase the use of spectrum sharing in both the government and the private sectors. The WSRD SSG continues to be guided by the following strategic objectives:

- *Transparency*: Communicate to both Federal agencies and the private sector the research and development activities currently being pursued or planned, and help identify areas that still need to be addressed

- *Smart investment*: Develop strategies that can supplement funding for research and development and/or increase the efficiency of existing investments

- *Solicit opportunities*: Identify opportunities for spectrum technology transfer between Federal agencies and the private sector

Current and Planned Coordination Activities

The WSRD SSG has developed a series of reports based on discussions at monthly meetings and four public-private workshops and, through data calls, created two inventories. The following summary highlights the SSG's activities and plans:

- In early 2011 the WSRD SSG created an inventory of over 600 Federal spectrum-sharing R&D projects. The inventory report, *Federal Spectrum Sharing Research Inventory*, is available on the NITRD website. A data call is underway to refresh and update the inventory in early 2014. The initial inventory prompted the first WSRD SSG workshop, held in July 2011, which engaged the academic and private sector communities in a dialogue about the Federal portfolio of research projects. The workshop report, *Toward Innovative Spectrum Sharing Technologies*, released in November 2011, reflects the recommendations and conclusions from the workshop

- Based on a second workshop held in January 2012, the WSRD SSG delivered the report, *Examining the Need for a National Spectrum Sharing Testing Environment* in September 2012. The report summarizes the group's findings and provides recommendations for the development of a national level spectrum-sharing testing facility coordination effort. Following up on these recommendations, the WSRD SSG created a unique online testbed information portal[16] that shows the locations and capabilities of existing spectrum testing facilities, and indicates the status and availability of each facility to Federal, academic, and private sector

---

[15] http://www.whitehouse.gov/the-press-office/presidential-memorandum-unleashing-wireless-broadband-revolution, Section 3.

[16] http://www.nitrd.gov/Subcommittee/wsrd/Testbeds/map.aspx

researchers. The testbed inventory was published through Data.gov in September 2013 in response to the June 14, 2013 *Presidential Memorandum – Expanding America's Leadership in Wireless Innovation*[17]

- A third workshop, held in July 2012, focused on collecting and exploring actual projects targeted to remove persistent barriers to spectrum-sharing adoption. In advance of the workshop, researchers submitted outlines of proposed research to help facilitate Executive, Congressional, and Agency mandates and goals in this area. Workshop participants, drawn from academia, the private sector, and the Federal Government, presented, discussed, and prioritized the proposals. This effort resulted in recommendations that the SSG delivered to OSTP in November 2012 in the report *Research Proposals that Facilitate Spectrum Sharing Adoption*

- A fourth workshop, held in April 2013, focused on the economic and policy research still needed to accelerate the adoption of spectrum-sharing technologies and facilitate technology transfer. Findings and recommendations were delivered to OSTP in December 2013 in the report, *Promoting Economic Efficiency in Spectrum Use: the economic and policy research agenda*

- A fifth workshop, "Spectrum Monitoring: Operations, Standards, and Enforcement Applications," is planned for late March 2014. The purpose of the workshop is to identify meaningful and achievable goals for spectrum monitoring that may improve spectrum utilization and to specify topics for research and standards that align with these goals

---

[17] http://www.whitehouse.gov/the-press-office/2013/06/14/presidential-memorandum-expanding-americas-leadership-wireless-innovatio, Section 2(b).

Faster Administration of Science and Technology Education and Research (FASTER)

Participating Agencies: DoD Service Research Organizations, DOE/SC, DHS, NARA, NASA, NIH, NIST, NOAA, NSF, OSD, and VA

The Federal CIO Council, under the leadership of OMB, coordinates the use of IT systems by Federal agencies. NITRD, under the leadership of OSTP, coordinates Federally supported IT research. The FASTER Community of Practice (CoP) is an association of science agency CIOs and/or their advanced technology specialists, organized under NITRD to improve the communication and coordination between the two interagency entities. The primary focus of FASTER is on the IT challenges specific to supporting the Federal scientific research enterprise.

Strategic Priorities

The FASTER CoP has identified several themes to promote the use of advanced IT systems in support of science agency research and development missions. Through coordination and collaboration, FASTER seeks to share information on protocols, standards, best practices, technology assessments, and testbeds, and to accelerate deployment of promising research technology. Consensus among the participants determines the focused theme activities. FASTER serves as a bridge between basic research and operational entities, especially in crosscutting domains. The group's activities are focused on the following strategic themes:

- Cloud computing
- Open government: open data and public access
- Accelerated communication

Current and Planned Coordination Activities

FASTER's goal is to enhance collaboration and accelerate agencies' adoption of advanced IT capabilities developed by government-sponsored IT research. FASTER hosts Emerging Technology workshops as well as monthly meetings with invited guest speakers to achieve this goal, including:

- *Cloud computing*: Focuses on issues regarding accessibility and equal access to information for all citizens. FASTER encourages collaboration between NIST and other Federal agencies to progress towards solutions in interoperability, portability, and security for cloud computing activities based on the high-priority requirements identified in the "US Government Cloud Computing Technology Roadmap" (NIST SP 500-293)

- *Open government*: Sponsors informal information-sharing exchanges and events that are responsive to shared interagency interests in Federal digital information sources, open data, and enhancing public access to Federally funded research results

- *Accelerated communication*: Promotes timely access to research results, technology assessments, and testbed results for the benefit of the IT operations community and broader audiences. FASTER communications promote the transition of promising technologies from research to practice and allow operational IT challenges and opportunities to be conveyed to the research community in a timely manner

NITRD Groups and Chairs

Interagency Working Group, Coordinating Group, and Team Chairs

Cyber Security and Information Assurance (CSIA) Interagency Working Group
Co-Chairs
Douglas Maughan, DHS
William D. Newhouse, NIST

High Confidence Software and Systems (HCSS) Coordinating Group
Co-Chairs
David Corman, NSF
William Bradley Martin, NSA
Albert J. Wavering, NIST

High End Computing (HEC) Interagency Working Group
*Co-Chairs**
Lucy Nowell, DOE/SC
Darren L. Smith, NOAA

Human-Computer Interaction and Information Management (HCI&IM) Coordinating Group
Co-Chairs
Leslie A. Collica, NIST
Sylvia Spengler, NSF

Large Scale Networking (LSN) Coordinating Group
Co-Chairs
Robert J. Bonneau, AFOSR
Vince Dattoria, DOE/SC
J. Bryan Lyles, NSF

LSN Teams:
Joint Engineering Team (JET)
Co-Chairs
Vince Dattoria, DOE/SC
Kevin Thompson, NSF
Middleware and Grid Interagency Coordination (MAGIC) Team
Co-Chairs
Daniel S. Katz, NSF
Richard Carlson, DOE/SC

Social, Economic, and Workforce Implications of IT and IT Workforce Development (SEW) Coordinating Group
Co-Chairs
C. Suzanne Iacono, NSF
Kevin Crowston, NSF

SEW Teams:
SEW-Collaboration Team
Co-Chairs
Kevin Crowston, NSF
Kara Hall, NCI

SEW-Education Team
Co-Chairs
Arlene de Strulle, NSF
Ernest McDuffie, NIST

Social Computing Team
Co-Chairs
Kevin Crowston, NSF
Rand Waltzman, DARPA

Software Design and Productivity (SDP) Coordinating Group
Co-Chairs
Ram D. Sriram, NIST
Sol Greenspan, NSF
James Kirby, NRL

Senior Steering Group, Subgroup, and Community of Practice Chairs

Big Data (BD) Senior Steering Group
Co-Chairs
C. Suzanne Iacono, NSF
Allen Dearry, NIH
George O. Strawn, NCO

Cyber Physical Systems (CPS) Senior Steering Group
Co-Chairs
Chris L. Greer, NIST
Keith Marzullo, NSF

Cybersecurity and Information Assurance (CSIA) Senior Steering Group
Co-Chairs
Keith Marzullo, NSF
Mark A. Luker, NCO

Health Information Technology R&D (HITRD) Senior Steering Group
Co-Chairs
Douglas B. Fridsma, ONC
Donald A.B. Lindberg, NIH
Howard D. Wactlar, NSF
George O. Strawn, NCO

HITRD Subgroup:
Health Information Technology Innovation and Development Environments (HITIDE) Subgroup
Co-Chairs
Mark Goodge, DoD/MHS
Vacant

Wireless Spectrum R&D (WSRD) Senior Steering Group
*Co-Chairs***
Byron Barker, NTIA
Mark A. Luker, NCO

Faster Administration of Science and Technology Education and Research (FASTER) Community of Practice (CoP)
Co-Chairs
Robert B. Bohn, NIST
Robert Chadduck, NSF

*John E. West, DoD (HPCMP), was Co-Chair of the HEC IWG through January 2014

**Andrew Clegg, formerly with NSF, was Co-Chair of the WSRD SSG through January 2014

Abbreviations and Acronyms

ACS – Advanced Computing Systems

AEH – Airborne electronic hardware

AFOSR – Air Force Office of Scientific Research

AFRL – Air Force Research Laboratory

AHRQ – HHS's Agency for Healthcare Research and Quality

ALCF – Argonne Leadership Computing Facility

ANI – Advanced Networking Initiative

ANL – DOE's Argonne National Laboratory

ARL – Army Research Laboratory

ARO – Army Research Office

ARSC – Arctic Region Supercomputing Center

ASC – DOE/NNSA's Advanced Simulation and Computing program

ASCR – DOE/SC's Advanced Scientific Computing Research

ASPR – Office of the Assistant Secretary for Preparedness and Response

ATC – Air traffic control

ATP – App Testing Portal

AWNS – DARPA's Advanced Wireless Networks for the Soldier program

BD – Big Data, one of NITRD's Senior Steering Groups

BD2K – NIH's Big Data to Knowledge program

BGPSEC – Border Gateway Protocol Security

BIRN – NIH's Biomedical Informatics Research Network

BISTI – NIH's Biomedical Information Science and Technology Initiative

BlueGene-Q – Latest-generation BlueGene architecture

BLS – U.S. Bureau of Labor Statistics

C3I – Communications, Command, Control, and Intelligence

CBIIT – NIH's Center for Biomedical Informatics and Information Technology

CCF – Computing and Communication Foundations

CC*IIE – NSF's Campus Cyberinfrastructure - Infrastructure, Innovation and Engineering program

CDC – Centers for Disease Control and Prevention

CDS&E – NSF's Computational and Data Sciences and Engineering program

CEMMSS – Cyber-enabled Manufacturing, Materials, and Smart Systems

CERDEC – U.S. Army's Communications-Electronics Research, Development, and Engineering Center

CG – Coordinating Group

CIF21 – NSF's Cyberinfrastructure Framework for 21st Century Science and Engineering program

CIO – Chief Information Officer

CISE – NSF's Computer and Information Science and Engineering directorate

CI TraCS – NSF's Fellowships for Transformative Computational Science using CyberInfrastructure

CMS – HHS's Centers for Medicare and Medicaid Services

CNCI – Comprehensive National Cybersecurity Initiative

COMPETES – Creating Opportunities to Meaningfully Promote Excellence in Technology, Education, and Science

CoP – Community of Practice

COTs – Commercial off-the-shelf technologies

CPS – Cyber-physical systems

CRASH – Clean-slate design of Resilient, Adaptive, Secure Hosts

CRUSHPROOF – Cyber Unification of Security Hardening and Protection of Operational Frameworks

CSIA – Cybersecurity and Information Assurance, one of NITRD's eight Program Component Areas

DARPA – Defense Advanced Research Projects Agency

DECIDE – Distributed Environment for Critical Infrastructure Decision-making Exercises

DEFIANT – Defensive Enhancements for Information Assurance Technologies

DETER – NSF- and DHS-initiated cyber Defense Technology Experimental Research testbed

DeVenCI – Defense Venture Catalyst Initiative

DHS – Department of Homeland Security

DIMRC – NIH's Disaster Information Management Research Center

DISA – Defense Information Systems Agency

DMZ – Demilitarized Zone; network architecture in which a security layer sits between a trusted, internal network and an untrusted, external network to protect access to the internal network

DNSSEC – Domain Name System Security Extensions

DOC – Department of Commerce

DoD – Department of Defense

DoD (HPCMP) – DoD's High Performance Computing Modernization Program

DoD/MHS – DoD's Military Health System

DoD/TATRC – DoD's Telemedicine and Advanced Technology Research Center

DOE – Department of Energy

DOE/INL – DOE's Idaho National Laboratory

DOE/NNSA – DOE's National Nuclear Security Administration

DOE/Oak Ridge – DOE's Oak Ridge National Laboratory

DOE/OE – DOE's Office of Electricity Delivery and Energy Reliability

DOE/SC – DOE's Office of Science

DOJ – Department of Justice

DOT – Department of Transportation

DPIF – Digital Preservation Interoperability Framework International Standard

DREN – DoD's Defense Research and Engineering Network

DTCN – DoD's (ONR) Dynamic Tactical Communications Networks

DTN – Delay-Tolerant Networking

E2E – End-to-End

EARS – Enhancing Access to the Radio Spectrum Program

ED – Department of Education

EHRs – Electronic health records

ENG – NSF's Engineering directorate

EPA – Environmental Protection Agency

ESG – Earth Systems Grid

ESMF – Earth System Modeling Framework

ESSC – DOE/SC's Energy Sciences network (ESnet) Steering Committee

FAA – Federal Aviation Administration

FASTER – NITRD's Faster Administration of Science and Technology Education and Research Community of Practice

FBI – Federal Bureau of Investigation

FCC – Federal Communications Commission

FDA – Food and Drug Administration

FHWA – Federal Highway Administration

FIA-NP – NSF's Future Internet Architectures – Next Phase program

FSSCC – Financial Services Sector Coordinating Council

FY – Fiscal Year

Gb – Gigabit

GENI – NSF's Global Environment for Networking Innovations program

GIS – Geographic Information System

GSA – General Services Administration

HCI&IM – Human-Computer Interaction and Information Management, one of NITRD's eight Program Component Areas

HCSS – High Confidence Software and Systems, one of NITRD's eight Program Component Areas

HEC – High End Computing

HEC I&A – HEC Infrastructure and Applications, one of NITRD's eight Program Component Areas

HEC R&D – HEC Research and Development, one of NITRD's eight Program Component Areas

HHS – Department of Health and Human Services

HITRD – Health Information Technology Research and Development, one of NITRD's Senior Steering Groups

HITIDE – HITRD SSG's Health Information Technology Innovation and Development Environments Subgroup

HOST – Homeland Open Security Technology

HPC – High-performance computing

HPCMP – DoD's High Performance Computing Modernization Program

HRD – NOAA's Hurricane Research Division

I/O – Input/output

IARPA – Intelligence Advanced Research Projects Activity

IATS – FHWA'S Integrated Active Transportation System

ICS – Industrial Control Systems

IETF – Internet Engineering Task Force

IHS – Indian Health Services

INCITE – DOE/SC's Innovative and Novel Computational Impact on Theory and Experiment program

InfiniBand – A switched fabric communications link used in high-performance computing and enterprise data centers

INRL – DOE's Idaho National Laboratory

Interior – Department of Interior

Internet2 – Higher-education consortium for advanced networking and applications deployment in academic institutions

IPv6 – Internet Protocol, version 6

IRNC – NSF's International Research Network Connections program

ISAP – Multiagency Information Security Automation Program

IT – Information technology

ITS – Institute of Telecommunications Science

ITSEF – Information Technology Security Entrepreneurs' Forum

IWG – Interagency Working Group

JET – LSN's Joint Engineering Team

JETnets – Federal research networks supporting networking researchers and advanced applications development

K-12 – Kindergarten through 12th grade

LANL – DOE's Los Alamos National Laboratory

LBNL – DOE's Lawrence Berkeley National Laboratory

LCF – DOE's Leadership Computing Facility

LLNL – DOE's Lawrence-Livermore National Laboratory

LSN – Large Scale Networking, one of NITRD's eight Program Component Areas

LTE – Long Term Evolution, a standard for wireless data communications technology

MAGIC – LSN's Middleware and Grid Interagency Coordination Team

MIC – Many integrated cores

MDAO – Multidisciplinary analysis optimization

META – DARPA's META program for model-based design and manufacturing

Morphinator – Morphing Network Assets to Restrict Adversarial Reconnaissance
MOU – Memorandum of Understanding
NARA – National Archives and Records Administration
NAS – NASA Advanced Supercomputing facility
NASA – National Aeronautics and Space Administration
NCAR – NSF-supported National Center for Atmospheric Research
NCBC – NIH's National Centers for Biomedical Computing
NCCS – NASA Center for Climate Simulation
NCI – NIH's National Cancer Institute
NCO – NITRD's National Coordination Office
NCR – National Cyber Range program
NERC-CIP – North American Electric Reliability Corporation's Critical Infrastructure Protection
NERSC – DOE/SC's National Energy Research Scientific Computing Center
NeTS – NSF's Networking Technology and Systems program
NextGen – Next Generation Air Transportation System
NEX – NASA Earth Exchange
NICE – National Initiative for Cybersecurity Education
NIGMS – NIH's National Institute of General Medical Sciences
NIH – National Institutes of Health
NIJ – DOJ's National Institute of Justice
NIST – National Institute of Standards and Technology
NITRD – Networking and Information Technology Research and Development
NLM – NIH's National Library of Medicine
NOAA – National Oceanic and Atmospheric Administration
NRC – Nuclear Regulatory Commission
NREIP – Naval Research Enterprise Summer Intern Program
NRI – National Robotics Initiative
NRL – Naval Research Laboratory
NSA – National Security Agency
NSF – National Science Foundation
NSF/MPS – NSF's Directorate for Mathematical and Physical Sciences
NSF/SBE – NSF's Directorate for Social, Behavioral, and Economic Sciences
NSTC – National Science and Technology Council
NSTIC – National Strategy for Trusted Identities in Cyberspace
NTIA – National Telecommunications and Information Administration
NTSB – National Transportation Safety Board
NTP – Network Time Protocol
N-Wave – NOAA's high speed network
ODNI – Office of the Director of National Intelligence
OFR – Treasury's Office of Financial Research
OLCF – Oak Ridge Leadership Computing Facility
OMB – White House Office of Management and Budget
ONC – HHS's Office of the National Coordinator for Health Information Technology
ONR – Office of Naval Research
OpenFlow – Open protocol for software-defined networks
OOMMF – Object-Oriented Micromagnetics Modeling Framework
ORCA – Online Representations and Certifications Application
ORNL – DOE's Oak Ridge National Laboratory
OS – Operating system

OSD – Office of the Secretary of Defense

OSG – Open Science Grid

OSTP – White House Office of Science and Technology Policy

PCA – Program Component Area

PCAST – President's Council of Advisors on Science and Technology

perfSONAR – performance Services-Oriented Network Architecture

PF – Petaflop(s), a thousand teraflops

PI – Principal investigator

PREDICT – DHS's Protected Repository for the Defense of Infrastructure Against Cyber Threats

QOS – Quality of Service

R&D – Research and development

RDT&E – DoD's Research Development Test & Evaluation programs

ROV – Remotely operated vehicle

RSIG – Remote Sensing Information Gateway

S&T – Science and technology

S4C – Science for Cybersecurity

S5 – Safe and Secure Software and Systems Symposium

SaTC – NSF's Secure and Trustworthy Cyberspace program

SAMATE – Software Assurance Metrics and Tool Evaluation

SATE – NIST's Static Analysis Tool Exposition

SBIR – Small Business Innovation Research, a Federal grant program

SCADA – Supervisory control and data acquisition

SCAP – Security Content Automation Protocol

SciDAC – DOE/SC's Scientific Discovery through Advanced Computing program

SDN – Software Defined Network

SDP – Software Design and Productivity, one of NITRD's eight Program Component Areas

SDSC – San Diego Supercomputer Center

SEI – Software Engineering Institute

SEES – NSF's Science, Engineering, and Education for Sustainability program

SensorWeb – NASA infrastructure of linked ground and space-based instruments to enable autonomous collaborative observation

SEW – Social, Economic, and Workforce Implications of IT and IT Workforce Development, one of NITRD's eight Program Component Areas

SEW-Ed – SEW's Education Team

SGIP – Smart Grid Interoperability Panel

SHARP – ONC's Strategic Health IT Advanced Research Projects

SI^2 – NSF's Software Infrastructure for Sustained Innovation

SME – Subject Matter Expert

SNL – Sandia National Laboratories

SSG – Senior Steering Group

State – Department of State

STEM – Science, technology, engineering, and mathematics

STONESOUP – IARPA's Security Taking on New Executable Software of Uncertain Provenance activity

SWAP – Size, Weight, And Power

TACC – Texas Advanced Computing Center

TCIPG – DHS- and DOE-supported Trustworthy Cyber Infrastructure Protection for the Power Grid program, with initial funding also from NSF

TeraGrid – NSF terascale computing grid, now succeeded by eXtreme Digital (XD) program

TF – Teraflop(s), a trillion floating-point operations per second

TIC – Trusted Internet Connection
TIES – DoD's Tactical Infrastructure Enterprise Services
TIS – NSF's XD Technology Insertion Service program
Treasury – Department of the Treasury
UAS – Unmanned Aircraft Systems
UAV – Unmanned aerial vehicle
UQ – Uncertainty quantification
USAF – United States Air Force
USAID – United States Agency for International Development
USDA – U.S. Department of Agriculture
USGCB – U.S. Government Configuration Baseline
USGS – U.S. Geological Survey
USHIK – United States Health Information Knowledgebase
VA – Department of Veterans Affairs
V&V – Verification and validation
VOSS – NSF's Virtual Organizations as Sociotechnical Systems program
VSTTE – Verified software, theories, tools, and experiments
VTC – Video Teleconferencing
WAIL – NSF's Wisconsin Advanced Internet Laboratory
WAN – Wide area network
WNaN – DARPA's Wireless Network after Next program
WSRD – Wireless Spectrum Research and Development, one of NITRD's Senior Steering Groups
XD – NSF's eXtreme Digital program
XSEDE – Extreme Science and Engineering Discovery Environment